✠ JOURNAL ✠

India:

WITH ✦ H.M.S. ✦ "SHANNON"
NAVAL BRIGADE,

From August 18th, 1858.

EDWARD SPENCER WATSON
NAVAL CADET.

Kettering:
W. E. AND J. GOSS, BOOKSELLERS AND STATIONERS.

INTRODUCTION

The existence of this Journal by Naval Cadet Edward S. Watson was unknown to Commander W.B. Rowbotham R.N. when he edited the definitive work *'The Naval Brigades in the Indian Mutiny 1857-58'* for the Navy Records Society in 1947. Whilst Major-General G.L. Verney made considerable use of Cadet Watson's letters to his mother in his story of H.M.S. *Shannon's* Naval Brigade, published in *'The Devil's Wind'* (Hutchinson 1956), this Cadet's Journal – covering the entire period this particular Naval Brigade was ashore – does not feature in his Bibliography.

Captain Oliver J. Jones R.N., who served in the Indian Mutiny as a 'Volunteer' with the 53rd Regiment, makes reference to the author of this Cadet's Journal in his *'Recollections of a Winter Campaign in India 1857-58'* (Saunders and Otley 1859) with the remarks that: '... Peel's two aides-de-camp, two fine little mids about 15 years old – Lascelles and Watson – by name, who used to stick to him like his shadow, under whatever fire he went, and seemed perfectly indifferent to the whizzing of bullets or the plunging of cannon-balls.' He might also have added that Lascelles was nearly a foot taller than the somewhat diminutive figure of Watson, who stood only 4 feet 5 inches in height.

Edward Spencer Watson, born in Rockingham Castle, Northants., joined the service aged 13 years as a Naval Cadet aboard H.M.S. *Shannon* on 11 September 1856. Promoted to Midshipman exactly two years later prior to his temporary appointment to H.M.S. *Victory* when *Shannon* was paid off on 15 January 1859. After serving five months aboard H.M.S. *Royal Albert* he was sent to H.M.S. *St. George* in June 1860 with the rank of Acting Sub Lieutenant, but resigned his Commission in the Royal Navy on 6 April 1863. He then transferred his allegiance to the Army, becoming a Cornet in the 10th (Prince of Wales's Own Regiment) Hussars with seniority of 12 June 1863 – receiving promotion to Lieutenant on 13 July 1867, but in the Spring of 1873 he resigned his Army Commission. He died in 1889.

As a tail-piece, the reader might like to know that the bookseller who sold this journal to me was unaware of my possession of Cadet Watson's Indian Mutiny Medal with its clasp 'Lucknow', which had been acquired at an auction some thirteen years earlier – both artifacts now reside with the Trustees of the Royal Navy Museum, Portsmouth.

June 1988. K.J.D-M.

AUGUST 18th, 1858, Tuesday, Calcutta.— All the arrangements for the departure of the Naval Brigade having been completed, we embarked to-day at one o'clock, on board the river steamer "Chunar" which is to take us up to Allahabad. Our party consists of 430 men, 50 of whom are marines, and 19 officers, including Captain Peel.

There is also a large flat which holds half the men and is also towed by the steamer. Captain Peel, five or six others including myself, and 200 men are on board the steamer, the rest are on board the flat. We have for passengers Colonel Otter, who is going up to take the command of the fort at Allahabad, and Lieutenant Parry, of the Madras Fusiliers, who is going to join his regiment up country. We have also a surgeon belonging to the East India Company attached to us, and who goes up with us in the steamer.

The Captain of the steamer is a rough kind of old customer, but seems good natured and anxious to make us as comfortable as he can during our passage up, which we expect will take us at least three weeks, as we have to anchor every night.

We all said good-bye to those who were left behind on board the ship without much regret, as we are all looking forward to the chance of active service when we get up country, but we all know that we shall be very lucky if we ever see the ship again, considering what we shall most probably have to go through before there is a chance of coming down again.

About half-past one this afternoon, we being all on board with baggage, &c., we tried to go ahead, but we found that although the steamer had only just had her engines repaired, they were still out of order, so we had to anchor for the night, and set some of our own stokers at work to see what they could do with her.

My baggage consists of a ship's black bag and a tin box, the former for my bedding, and the latter for my kit, which is not very extensive. I found to my disgust about eight o'clock this evening that my bag with the bedding in it had been taken on board the flat instead of the steamer, and as we had cast off and anchored some little way down the river, I was not able to get it, and had to content myself with sleeping on the deck outside the saloon.

August 19th, Wednesday.—At nine o'clock this morning we weighed anchor, the engines having been repaired in the night. We anchored last night a little astern of the "Shannon," so we consequently had to pass her on her way up. As we passed her, we saw all the men and officers we had left behind standing up on the hammock netting as they were too few to man the rigging, and they gave us three cheers which we replied to. We next passed the "Pearl," the only other man-of-war at Calcutta,

She manned rigging, gave us three cheers, and fired a salute of seven guns. The merchant ships all dipped their colours, and all those who could muster enough men cheered us and paid us every respect possible. We had to anchor again to-day about twelve o'clock, much to our disgust, as there was a strong current running, and the "Chunar" being a wretched steamer could not stem it.

August 20th, Thursday.—We started again the first thing this morning, and arrived again at Barrackpore about ten o'clock. We anchored here, and Captain Peel, being already quite disgusted with this wretched steamer, telegraphed to Calcutta asking them to send up the American steamer "River Bird" to take us on. We are all glad of this, as its very evident we shall never get to Allahabad at this rate.

August 21st, Friday.—At twelve o'clock to-day we saw the "River Bird" steaming up the river towards us, and she lashed alongside of us at once. We immediately began shifting over to her. We found her a much larger and more comfortable vessel than the "Chunar." She has a large saloon, beautifully fitted up, and the captain seems a very nice, gentlemanly fellow. We are all very pleased at the change. About two o'clock, after taking the flat in tow again, we started and left the "Chunar" to her fate. She will go down again to Calcutta either this evening or to-morrow morning. We anchored at dusk off Chandernagore. The "River Bird" steams capitally, and we are all excessively comfortable. The saloon is fitted up with sofas all round on which we make up our beds. The captain also messes us capitally.

August 22nd, Saturday.—We weighed anchor at five

o'clock this morning. About nine o'clock we entered the part of the Ganges called the Bhangarathy, and left the Hooghly. To-day we began excercising the men at drill. There is not much room for them on deck, but Captain Peel is determined to keep their drill up. We anchored at dusk off Nudya.

August 23rd, Sunday.—We weighed at daylight this morning. Had church at ten o'clock, and anchored again at dusk. It has been raining almost the whole day, and the river looks very high, and in some places is regularly flooding the country.

August 24th, Monday.—Weighed anchor at daylight. Exercised the men at drill in the morning, anchored about six o'clock this evening a little below Beerhampoor, which we expect to reach early to-morrow morning.

August 25th, Tuesday.—We weighed about half-past five this morning, and anchored off Beerhampoor at six o'clock. We landed all the men both from the flat and from the steamer almost immediately on our arrival for drill. Our two field pieces were also landed, and the men seemed to enjoy it very much, and drilled capitally, considering that they had not all been drilled together before. Beerhampoor seems rather a nice place. A detachment of the 35th is stationed there, and they have got a very good cricket ground. Comerford, our assistant paymaster, and myself went on shore in hopes of getting a game of cricket with them, but it came on to rain as soon as we got on shore and we had to give it up. Mr. Bowman went out snipe shooting, but came back with only one snipe and very wet. The 63rd native infantry and a regiment of irregular cavalry who showed signs of mutiny and were disarmed some time ago are also here We do not know for certain how long we shall be detained here, as the pilot objects to take us up any farther, and so we may perhaps have to wait until the "Mirzapore" arrives. She is expected down shortly to take us up.

August 26th, Wednesday.—We landed both our field pieces early this morning for drill. They were left on shore during the day, and brought on board again this evening. Captain Peel has been talking to the pilot almost all day, and has at last persuaded him to take us up farther, although he says it is running a great risk, as no steamer drawing more water than the "River Bird" has ever been higher up the river than Beerhampoor.

August 27th, Thursday. Weighed anchor at daylight this morning, passed Moorshedabad about nine o'clock, and also two steamers going down the river. We anchored for the night about four o'clock this afternoon off Jungypore.

August 28th, Friday.—Weighed anchor about a quarter-past five this morning. About seven o'clock we touched the ground, but we backed out and got clear without injury. To-day we left the Bhangarathy and entered the Ganges again. The captain made us all fall in to-day and have some drill which is rather pleasant than otherwise, as we have nothing else to do. Anchored for the night about half-past six.

August 29th, Saturday.—At about half-past four this morning, William Claxton (ords. seaman) fell overboard as he was crossing over from this steamer to the flat. It was pitch dark and blowing very hard at the time, and as the current was very strong, little hopes were entertained for his recovery. We immediately sent a boat and lowered cable so as to drop down nearer to him, but he was soon lost in the darkness, and although we hailed several times, we could hear nothing of him. At last, after waiting for about half an hour, the boat returned with the man safe. He had been carried down the river for about a quarter of a mile by the current, but he luckily drifted against a sand bank, which he held on to till the boat came up. Captain Peel was so pleased at the man being brought back safe, that he noted all the men that were in the boat, and congratulated both the officers that were in her. About half-past six we went on again, and anchored for the night at about half-past seven this evening off Rajamahal.

August 30th, Sunday.—Weighed at five o'clock this morning and had service both on board the steamer and the flat. The flat is now lashed alongside of us, instead of astern, which makes it very convenient, as we can easily cross over. Anchored for the night about half-past seven off the mouth of the Parssomtea Nullah.

August 31st, Monday.—Weighed anchor about half-past five this morning, and sighted the Himalaya mountains; they were said to be about 200 miles off. At seven o'clock we grounded on a sand bank, and the current being against us, we bumped tremendously, and parted several of the hawsers by which the flat was made fast to us, but after a little difficulty we succeeded in backing off and were obliged to anchor, as some sand had got into the engines and prevented them from working. About eight o'clock, the engines being clear, we weighed anchor and went on again. Had some musket drill in the morning. Passed the Colgony rocks about half-past four this afternoon. These rocks are considered very dangerous, and steamers continually run aground there, so we considered ourselves very lucky in getting through all safe, especially as we draw more water than any other steamer that has ever been up here. Anchored for the night about half-past seven off Balropore.

September 1st, Tuesday.—Weighed anchor this morning at five o'clock. Passed Bangulpore about half-past six. About half-past eight we observed a steamer aground close to the bank of the river: she had evidently been trying to make a short cut. She proved to be the "Calcutta" with a detachment of the 90th regiment on board. We were too far off to render her any assistance. We passed the steamer "Benares" going down the river with two flats in tow about ten o'clock. Anchored for the night about seven o'clock this evening.

September 2nd, Wednesday.—Weighed at about five o'clock this morning. Had some musket drill. Arrived at Monghir about half-past two this afternoon, and after coaling went on again about four o'clock, and anchored for the night a little way off from the town.

September 3rd, Thursday.—Weighed at five o'clock this morning. One of our men named Daniel Richard died this morning of fever. We anchored about six o'clock this evening off a small village called Durriapore, where we had the funeral. The whole of our men were landed and we buried him in a beautiful place under a large tree close to where an officer had been buried twenty years before, who died on his way down the river. We had to march for about half a mile to the burial ground, our band playing the Dead March, and we were followed by a great many of the villagers, who collected round us, but seemed more frightened of the ceremony than otherwise. We got on board again about half-past seven.

September 4th, Friday.—Weighed anchor at about half-past five this morning, and anchored for the night at dusk 18 miles below Dinapoor, which place we expect to reach to-morrow, and we hope to find the steamer "Mirzapore" waiting for us, as it will be an impossibility for the steamer to go up any further.

September 5th, Saturday.—Weighed anchor at about half-past five this morning. Arrived at Dinapoor at four o'clock this afternoon, but found that the "Mirzapore" has not yet arrived, so we are to go on shore to barracks and await her arrival, and the "River Bird" is to go down again to Calcutta immediately before the river begins to fall. We landed the whole of our men this evening at five o'clock, and drilled them on the parade ground. Dinapoor is a large town with a good many Europeans in it. H.M. 10th regiment are stationed here now.

September 6th, Sunday.—We began clearing out of the steamer the first thing this morning, and marched the men up to barracks. Our own quarters are very miserable: two large rooms with a large bare table in each, and a few miserable forms. The 10th have made us honorary members of their mess, so we shall always mess with them. Captain Peel has taken up his quarters with the colonel of the 10th. Dined with the 10th this evening. They have got a very good mess, and seem all very good fellows.

September 7th, Monday.—Exercised at drill at five o'clock this morning. This is the only time except in the evening which we can drill the men in, as it is too hot during the day. The steamer "Calcutta" arrived this morning with some Madras Fusiliers, who are to be landed. We had more drill this evening, the captain is determined to give them plenty of it now he has got the chance.

September 8th, Tuesday.—Drill at five o'clock this morning and again in the evening. Captain Peel is getting very impatient at being delayed. Steamers arrive every now and then, but have not as yet brought any news of the "Mirzapore."

September 9th, Wednesday.—Drill at daylight this morning. One of our men was taken with cholera to-day. This was the first case we have had. Several of the men are on the sick list with sore feet. The reason is that they have to drill with their shoes on, which they have never been used to, and their feet get blistered.

September 10th, Thursday.—No news of the Mirzapore yet. There is a rumour that 10,000 sepoys are marching on this place, but we do not yet know anything for certain. My foot, which has been bad for some time, has got rather worse to-day, and I was obliged to go to the doctor. He put some dressing on, but if it does not soon get better, I shall have to go on the sick list. It originated from my scratching some mosquito bites on my foot, and it has festered.

September 11th, Friday.—At last the "Mirzapore" has arrived. We embarked the sick and baggage to-day, and we are to embark ourselves to-morrow.

September 12th, Saturday.—Embarked on board the "Mirzapore" the first thing this morning, and started about twelve o'clock, after having taken the flat in tow. We left four or five men behind us in hospital. About half-past six this evening we had to come to an anchor, only having gone six miles the whole day, the current being very strong. We sent a boat down to Dinapoor to request the authorities there to send us up the steamer "Coel" which was at anchor there to assist us in towing up the flat.

September 13th, Sunday.—Our request was complied with, and the "Coel" arrived at daylight this morning. She made fast on one side of the flat, and we on the other. Started about seven o'clock and anchored this evening near Chupra. Three cases of cholera occurred during the afternoon.

September 14th, Monday.—Weighed early this morning. We find the steamer very uncomfortable. The engines are just outside the doors of a small saloon where we live, and the mosquitoes are something fearful, and we are hardly able to get a wink of sleep all night. My foot is much worse, and I am now on the sick list, and hardly able to walk. One of our men named ——— died to-day of cholera and was committed to the river in the evening.

September 15th, Tuesday.—Weighed early this morning but had to anchor again soon afterwards, the current being too strong. One of our men named Cornelius Collins died of cholera to-day, and we buried him in the evening.

September 16th, Wednesday.—Passed the mouth of

the river Gogra, and anchored again about dusk. The current is still running very strong, and the weather very hot.

September 17th, Thursday.—Weighed early this morning. Ran aground about half past nine, and all our attempts to get her off failed ; but as a last resource we shifted all the shot aft, and being thus made lighter she floated off. Anchored for the night.

September 18th, Friday.—Started again early this morning. About ten o'clock this morning there was a partial eclipse of the sun. A man named Coleman and a marine named Woods both died to-day of cholera, and we buried them in the evening. Anchored for the night off Malaychur.

September 19th, Saturday.—Weighed early this morning. Ran on shore about half-past two this afternoon, and stuck hard and fast. We were trying to make a short cut, and are now hard and fast close to the bank of the river, and as the river is falling fast, there is a very poor chance of our getting off. The " Coel " and the flat cast off when we ran aground and went on for a mile farther up.

September 20th, Sunday.—The " Coel " came down again this morning to see if she could offer us any assistance, but it was to no purpose, so she lashed alongside of us and took all our shot on board. Captain Peel and Lascelles then went on board of her, and they are gone on with the flat to Ghazeepoor, which is the next town we come to, leaving Lieutenant Wilson, Mr. Bowman, and two or three others, including myself. If we are unable to get off, the " Coel " is to land the men she has now on board at Ghazeepoor, and then come down and take us up, leaving the "Mirzapore" to her fate. The reason I was left behind was on account of my foot, which is still bad, and I am obliged to keep as quiet as possible to prevent the inflammation on it from getting worse. We have been employed the whole day trying to get her off, but it is no use. This evening the "Bombay," one of the river steamers, came down and anchored a little way astern. One of the mates came on board and offered us assistance if the captain of the "Mirzapore" would give 800 rupees a day for his trouble, which he consented to do, and they agreed to assist us in the morning.

September 21st, Monday.—At daylight this morning we observed the "Bombay" steaming full speed down the river, although having promised us assistance the night before. We are all in a great rage about it, and the captain of the steamer intends to bring an action against the captain of the "Bombay" for doing it. We have been trying all we can to get her off to-day but to no purpose. The river has fallen so much that on one side we are high and dry against the bank of the river. The vessel is in a very uncomfortable position, being all over on one side, and as there is a slight chance of her capsizing altogether, we got a sail on shore and rigged up a kind of tent, to which we shall have to go if she goes over. We easily step on shore from the deck, and as there are supposed to be some sepoys near, we have served out ammunition to all the men and loaded our pistols, lest if they should hear of our position, they should take advantage of it and attack us. We are now about ten miles from the place where some of the 10th regiment were defeated and almost all killed by the sepoys at the commencement of the mutiny.

September 22nd, Tuesday.—We are still in the same position, and have some natives digging under the paddle boxes, which are quite buried in the ground. The jackals came close up last night, and some of them came almost on board making a most terrific yelling.

September 23rd, Wednesday.—To-day the "Coel" came down again with Captain Peel, and we all embarked on board of her. She arrived all safe at Ghazeepoor, and landed the rest of our fellows there. We hear that the officers have got very nice quarters in an officer's private house, who has gone up country.

September 24th, Thursday.—We weighed early this morning, anchored for the night about five miles below Buxar.

September 25th, Friday.—Weighed at daylight this morning, anchored at Buxar about ten o'clock, took some bread on board, and went on again. Anchored for the night a little below Ghazeepoor.

September 26th, Saturday.—Arrived at Ghazeepoor about eight o'clock this morning and found the flat here but quite empty, all the men being on shore at barracks. We landed this evening, and Doctor Brale drove me up to our quarters in a dog-cart he had lent to him.

I found all the rest of our fellows here. We are in a very nice quarter: a nice house, garden, and swimming bath attached, belonging to Captain Innis, who is at Allahabad. Our men are in the barracks which are close to. Captain Peel and all but our party who were left in the "Mirzapore" go on to Allahabad to-morrow in the

"Coel," and we are to remain here until she returns after landing them. My foot still bad, and this is the reason I am left behind again.

September 27th, Sunday.—The "Coel" started early this morning with Captain Peel and party, but returned again in a few hours and anchored opposite our bungalow, not having been able to stem the current, so she is going to land about 70 tons of shot and leave them here until she comes back again, when she will be able to take them up, as the flat will be left at Allahabad. Had service in the barracks. Captain Peel came up to our bungalow to-day, he is very much disappointed at not being able to get on.

September 28th, Monday.—The "Coel" started again this morning, but on taking the flat in tow again, found she could not make headway against the current, although she was so much lighter, and she was forced to anchor about a mile up the river. About one hour after, we observed the "Mirzapore" steaming up the river, and Clinton was immediately sent in a boat up to the "Coel" to inform Captain Peel of the fact. He got almost alongside of her, but the current carried the boat down and he missed her, but never thought of shouting out to the captain his message while he was drifting past her, and consequently they would have been left in total ignorance of the "Mirzapore's" arrival if they had not happened to see the smoke and guessed that she was there. The captain was in a great way with Clinton about this, but they made it up all right soon afterwards. As soon as the "Mirzapore" arrived, she took in all the shot that the "Coel" had landed, but as she is not to take any men, we are all to be left behind here, which we do not mind at all, as we are much more comfortable than we should be on board the steamer. Our party consists of Mr. Wilson, who is in command, Mr. Bowman, Mr. Quid, Comerford, Dr. Brale, Clinton, and myself. Captain Peel intends starting to-morrow morning.

September 29th, Tuesday.—Captain Peel, with the two steamers and flat, started this morning, and were soon out of sight. Received the intelligence of the capture of Delhi by General Wilson, with the loss of 600 men killed and 29 officers, and 39 of the latter wounded. General Havelock has marched on Lucknow, and heavy firing has been heard in that direction, but nothing known yet for certain. Went for a drive with Captain Jackson, who is commandant stud here, and is very kind to us, and as I am not able to walk about in the day-time, on account of my foot, a drive was very welcome, and I enjoyed it very much.

September 30th, Wednesday.—To-day we received an invitation to dine from the officers of the 37th regiment. Mr. Bowment, Comerford, and Clinton are going. Drove with Mr. Bowman to Lord Cornwallis's tomb, which was erected by the inhabitants of Calcutta. It is well worth seeing, and has a nice garden all round it, which is very well kept. The top of it was crowded with wild pigeons, and Mr. Bowman had some shots at them, and killed two, which we had for dinner in the evening.

October 1st, Thursday.—A report is flying about to-day, about some Sepoys who are expected to attack this place. As all the sick men, about 50 in number, are with us, it would be rather awkward if they were to attempt it, as we have not got many men, and should be obliged to depend on the hospital alone.

October 2nd, Friday.—The men marched out this evening and had some rifle practice. The weather is fearfully hot, and a good many of them are falling sick.

October 3rd, Saturday.—Found this morning that Mr. Bowman's desk had been broken open during the night, and that about 100 rupees had been stolen out of it. The native police have been told of it, but the culprits have not yet been discovered. Heard that Mr. Vaughan with 4 officers and 140 newly raised seamen have left Calcutta on their way to join us.

October 4th, Sunday.—Had divine service in the barracks this morning. A steamer passed us to-day with some Madras Fusiliers on board.

October 5th, Monday.—Observed the steamer "Coel" steaming down for us, about five o'clock this evening. When she arrived the captain came on shore and said he was all ready to take us on, and that he had landed Captain Peel and the rest at Allahabad, where they were quartered in the fort. We are to embark the first thing to-morrow morning.

October 6th, Tuesday.—Embarked the men on board the "Coel" about seven o'clock this morning. We had some difficulty in getting the sick on board, but we managed to get away about half-past nine this morning. Anchored in the evening after having grounded once, but we got off without injury.

October 7th, Wednesday.—The master-at-arms died to-day about half-past twelve. He is a great loss, especially as the master-at-arms has so much to do with the discipline and order of the men, and he was such an excellent one and liked by all. He had been ill of dysentery for a long while. We buried him on shore. Arrived at Benares, and came to anchor for the purpose of coaling. After filling up with coals, went on again, and passed the fort of "Chunar," a large fort which was taken by our troops from the Sepoys, and is now used as an invalid depot for the use of men coming down from up country sick, and who are not able to obtain a passage down. Anchored for the night about fifteen miles below Dinapore off a place called Battowbigot.

October 8th, Thursday.—Weighed about six o'clock this morning. A man named Guines died to-day, and we buried him this evening. About nine o'clock this morning we stopped a little below Mirzapore, and lashed to the bank of the river, opposite a coaling depot, where we completed our complement of coals, and then went on again. Anchored for the night below Deeza.

October 9th, Friday.—Weighed at day-light. During the night a seaman named Thomas died, and we landed a party on shore this morning and buried him. About half-past eight we came to a very difficult passage, considered to be the most dangerous place in the river, the channel being marked with bamboos stuck in the water. We had to anchor, and sent our pilot with some native boatmen on ahead to sound, but they could not find more than three and three quarters feet of water, whereas we draw four feet, so we were obliged to lay out the anchors and try and heave her over. After working the whole day, we managed to get over the shoal about eight o'clock this evening, just as it was getting dark. A very heavy thunder storm passed over us with heavy rain. Anchored for the night as soon as we got off.

October 10th, Saturday.—At daylight weighed anchor. Met the "Mirzapore" steaming downwards about eight o'clock this morning, she hailed us as she passed, and said that they were in great want of troops at Allahabad, and that she was going down to Benares for some. We arrived at Allahabad at about half-past three this afternoon, and in the evening took up our quarters in the right wing of the barracks in the fort. Captain Peel is at present commandant here, and our men mount guard and garrison the whole place. Most of the men are getting the heavy 68-pounders out of the flat, they have not cleared her yet.

October 11th, Sunday.—Performed divine service in barracks this morning. We all form one large mess together now.

October 12th, Monday.—The 93rd Highlanders arrived to-day and encamped outside the fort. My foot is at last all right again, and I am now out of the sick list and able to get about again. There is a large fort on the opposite side of the river nearly in ruins, but would make a capital position for the enemy if they attempted to attack this place, and as there is some likelihood of it, the captain went over to examine it and see whether it would be worth while to garrison it, but I do not know the result of his excursion.

October 13th, Tuesday.—Our men are still at work getting our guns out of the flat. Three officers and about 50 men of the East India Company arrived to-day in a gunboat and we sent our band down to meet them, and have made them honorary members of our mess for the time that they remain here. They dined with us this evening. Lieutenant Parry, who came up with us this evening in the steamer, has left us and gone up with a detachment of his regiment to Lucknow.

October 16th, Friday.—To-day one of our midshipmen named E. St. John Daniels went up to Cawnpore on special service to take charge of a small battery there. They are in great want of artillery officers there, and he has been sent up to supply the deficiency. He went up with a detachment of the 53rd regiment.

October 17th, Saturday.—We heard the news to-day of the relief of Lucknow by General Havelock, and we also have received a list of those who were found alive in the garrison. Among them is the name of a brother of one of our lieutenants. Brigadier Campbell of the Queen's Bays arrived to-day and took command of the fort instead of Captain Peel. We expect soon to move up.

October 18th, Sunday.—Had church this morning at the barracks.

October 19th, Monday.—The officers and men of the Indian Navy who joined us the other day have received orders to go down the river as far as Benares in their gunboat, for service in the river Gogra. They embark this evening, and start to-morrow morning.

October 20th, Tuesday.—Lieutenant Vaughan with five officers and about 120 newly raised merchant seamen arrived this afternoon in the steamer "Benares." We all marched down to the river side to receive them, and marched into barracks with them. Before dismissing the men, Captain Peel gave a short speech, and the men gave three cheers. Although this last party did not leave Calcutta till a month after we did, they have arrived almost as soon, as they have had no accidents or difficulties to contend with on their way up like we had. They have had a sergeant of the 78th Highlanders to drill them on their way up in the steamer, and they seem to be very well up in it. Lieutenant Wilson is for the future to have command of them, and they are to be called the first company, They are all armed with Enfield rifles. Lieutenant Vaughan will most probably be sent up the country with the first party that goes up.

October 21st, Wednesday.—This afternoon all the men that arrived yesterday were moved outside the fort, and the captain received them. They went through all the drill very well. and the captain was much pleased with them.

October 22nd, Thursday.—To-day Lieutenant Vaughan and four officers, Lieutenant Sabraon, Daniels, Kerr, and Clinton (the latter three midshipmen), left barracks and encamped outside the fort, close to the railway station, and to-morrow they are to start for Cawnpore with some of the 93rd Highlanders. They have with them four 24-pounders, belonging to the prize train. The 68-pounders which we brought up from the ship are considered too heavy for service in the field, and are to be left in the fort.

October 23rd, Friday.—This morning, early, Lieutenant Vaughan and party started for Cawnpore. They are to go up by train for about 50 miles; they then encamp and commence their marches, of which they will have seven or eight before they reach their destination. The company that started this morning are the 2nd, formerly under command of Lieutenant Sabraon, but Lieutenant Vaughan is now put in command of the whole party going up. There are a party of thirty men with them (besides the second company, called field-piece men).

October 24th, Saturday.—Another party of our men with some guns were to have started this afternoon, but in consequence of the guns not being ready for them, they are to be delayed until next Monday or Tuesday. A most alarming report was spread to-day that Delhi had been re-taken by the rebels. We do not yet know if it is true or not, but it is not at all unlikely as we have very few men holding the place, and the enemy are swarming all round them.

October 25th, Sunday.—Had church in the barracks this morning, after which we heard that the report about Delhi being re-taken was not true, and that a spy who had brought the news had been well flogged.

October 26th, Monday.—The guns being all ready. Lieutenant Young and his party marched outside the fort, accompanied by the Marines, and encamped near the railway station, ready for starting to Cawnpore, to-morrow morning.

October 27th, Tuesday.—Lieutenant Young and his party left this morning. We hear that we are to march to-morrow, and we have been employed all the afternoon loading carts with baggage, &c., and sending them down to the railway station. The captain asked Lascelles and myself if we had rather remain behind with some of the men who were going to be left, or still remain as his aides-de-camp and go on with him. We of course told him we preferred going on with him, which he assented to, although he did not seem very anxious to take us up.

October 28th, Wednesday.—This afternoon the 3rd company, consisting of 86 men and 10 officers, Captain Peel, Lieutenant Hay, Garvey (mate), Mr. Bowman, the chaplain, Lascelles and myself among the number, left the fort, and marched out to the railway station. We left behind us the 1st company, who are all men lately raised from the merchant service, at Calcutta, under Lieutenant Wilson, and also a few other men under command of Lieutenant Lurid (the Swedish lieutenant). Lieutenant Wilson is in command of all those left. We started by rail at about ten o'clock, but before we had gone far an alarm of fire was given and we had to stop. We all bundled out at once, and found that some trucks full of tentage and stores had caught fire, and were already smoking. As there were some trucks full of ammunition close by, there was no time to lose, and everything had to be cleared out. After about half an hour's work the fire was extinguished. All that was good for anything was restored, and we went on again, having stationed a man with a loaded musket on each truck to give an alarm if he saw anything of a fresh outbreak. We are in company with a detachment of the 23rd Royal Welsh Fusiliers and the Royal Engineers. The former have got a large goat which was presented to them by the Queen, and which always follows the regiment wherever it goes. At about seven o'clock we arrived at Suhunda, and I went with the captain to choose the ground for our first encampment. We were some time pitching the tents, as our men are not used yet to this kind of work. As we had no way of getting any grub, we were obliged to content ourselves with some biscuits, a box of which I had luckily bought at Allahabad, and some tea, but afterwards having got at our stock of provisions, we had some preserved soup. Mr. Bowman, Lascelles, Munro (the interpreter), and myself are in a tent together, and we have already managed to make ourselves pretty comfortable.

October 29th, Thursday.—Lieutenant Young and some of the fellows who went up with him, and were encamped about a mile and a half off, came over to see us this morning, and we joined them this afternoon. We found them encamped at a dak bungalow, which is a kind of half way house by the side of the grand trunk road. We also found detachments of several regiments with them, under command of Captain Cox of the 75th regiment.

October 30th, Friday.—The whole force struck tents and started on the march at one o'clock this morning. We arrived at our camping ground at six o'clock this morning, just as the sun was coming out, and pitched tents. We are of course much longer than the soldiers pitching them, but our men will soon get into the way of it. We were joined soon after our arrival by three companies of the 53rd regiment under Captain Powell, who, at Captain Peel's request, assumed the command of the whole force.

October 31st, Saturday.—We struck tents and started on the march at two o'clock this morning, and arrived at our next camping ground about eight o'clock, after a march of 13 miles. About 4.30 this afternoon orders came, to our astonishment, to strike tents at once, and a report soon spread that we were to attack a force of Sepoys who were said to be somewhere in the neighbourhood. We arrived at Futtehpoor at half-past twelve at night, when we heard that the enemy were in force about 24 miles off, and that we were to attack them in the morning.

November 1st, Sunday.—Our tents did not arrive until half-past two this morning, so we had to content ourselves by making a fire and lying down on the bare ground until they came up. This delay was not very pleasant, as the night was cold with a heavy dew falling. At three o'clock this morning, the party of our men to go with the attacking force were told off. It was arranged that the six siege train guns we have with us were to be left behind in the camp with about 50 of our men, 150 soldiers, and all the sick. To our great disappointment the captain would not allow either Lascelles or myself to go. Four officers went, that is Sterling (the Marine officer), Lieutenant Hay, Garvey, and Bone. They started about four o'clock, leaving Lieutenant Young, Bowman (the chaplain), Grey (captain of Marines), two or three other midshipmen, Lascelles and myself behind. The force consists, in addition to our men, of one company of the Royal Engineers, two companies of the 53rd, a company of the 93rd Highlanders, and about 60 men of different regiments: not a very large force considering that the Sepoys are said to be the Durapore mutineers, 2000 strong, and with several guns. Powell of the 53rd commands our force. We remained the whole day in a state of the greatest excitement and suspense, reports and rumours of all sorts constantly coming in. In the afternoon we heard for certain that our men had come up with the enemy and had engaged them, but we could get no reliable account of what took place afterwards. About 12.30 we were lying down quietly in our tents, when to our surprise the alarm sounded. We immediately fell in, all the available men loaded the guns, and threw our skirmishers in all directions to reconnoitre. Bowman, the chaplain, sallied out with his double-barrelled gun and dog " Pilot " to see what could be seen, and we expected every instant to hear the skirmishers open fire. It, however, all came to nothing, as no signs of an enemy were discovered. The alarm came first from a guard tent a little way outside the camp, and some of the men there declared they had seen a body of armed Sepoys not far off marching towards the camp. After having satisfied ourselves that the alarm was false, the men were dismissed, all much amused at the adventure, but had the alarm proved true, we should have found ourselves rather in a fix, with so few men, and the whole camp with the siege train and camp to protect. In the evening we heard that Colonel Powell, who commanded our force, had been shot dead at the commencement of the action, and that Captain Peel, who ranks with a full colonel, had taken the command, also that one of our officers had been severely wounded.

November 2nd, Monday.—This morning we got an account of yesterday's action. Our men came up with the enemy after a march of 24 miles, and found them in a strong position near a village called Kudjwa. After a desperate fight which lasted four or five hours, we defeated the enemy, killing three or four hundred of them, including their commander. Colonel Powell was shot through the head at the commencement of the action, and the whole action afterwards was fought under the command of our captain. The enemy fought desperately. Sterling, the Marine officer, was shot through the calf of his leg, and Hay, one of our lieutenants, was slightly wounded in the hand. The men returned about eight o'clock this evening with lots of loot of all kinds, including some ponies, &c., and in high spirits. Our total loss was 96 killed and wounded. Three of our own sailors were killed and several wounded. Captain Peel is much pleased with this the first action the Naval Brigade have taken part in, and with the behaviour of the men.

November 3rd, Tuesday.—A quiet day in camp to rest the men after yesterday.

November 4th, Wednesday.—The 23rd regiment marched into the fort at Futtehpoor this morning. This afternoon we started again and encamped about nine p.m., after a long march.

November 5th, Thursday.—Started again this afternoon and marched to a place called Agoung. Our marches are generally for about twelve or fifteen miles, and our men are now getting pretty used to them, though at first they used to get dreadfully footsore and knocked up.

November 6th, Friday.—Off at three o'clock this morning, and encamped again at a place called Rajpore, about 9.30. At half-past twelve struck tents again, and marched for Cawnpore, where we arrived at half-past six in the evening, and encamped at the cantonments close to General Wheeler's entrenchment which he held so long against the mutineers. I went to see the latter place soon after we arrived. The walls are almost all knocked down, and there are shot holes through about every twelve inches of those walls that are standing. Our men are to move on to Lucknow, with the exception of a party of 50, who are to be left behind here to garrison the fort. The officers are to be Hay, Garvey, Lascelles, and myself. The captain came to our tent to-day, and had a long talk with Lascelles and myself, when he said that he was very sorry to be unable to take us with him, but as we were so young, he could not undertake the responsibility of doing so. We were much disappointed at this, as of course we expected that having taken us with him away from the ship, we should go everywhere with him; we, however, could not get him to alter his mind. The only thing we could get out of him was that if we came in for any fighting here and got our heads knocked off, it would be all right, but that he would not have the responsibility of taking us needlessly into great danger. No doubt being in attendance on him under heavy fire, we should run a great risk, but we naturally consider that he might have thought of that before, and not waited till our expectations were raised.

November 7th, Saturday.—We struck tents at six o'clock this morning, and marched across the river, encamping again about two miles the other side of it.

November 8th, Sunday.—The captain with the whole of the brigade, except the party of 50 left behind with us, started for Lucknow at four o'clock this morning, and we returned broken hearted to the entrenched camp at

Cawnpore, where we were to remain. We however have some hopes of getting an opportunity of distinguishing ourselves here, as we are quite likely to be attacked. The men were put under canvas in the entrenched camp. A Mr. Moore, a missionary chaplain, a very good hospitable fellow, offered both board and lodging in his bungalow to both Lascelles and myself, and as our duties did not prevent our doing so, we accepted his kind offer, and established ourselves under his roof. A very good natured sort of fellow, Dangerfield, in the Madras Fusiliers, was also staying with him, and we soon made great friends.

November 9th, Monday.—Lieutenant Hay, who commands our party, is very unwell with fever, and to-day unable to get up. Troops have been passing through on their way to the relief of Lucknow the whole day.

November 10th, Tuesday.— We marched out for exercise about 6.30 this morning, and on our way met General Wyndham who is in command here. He is very popular, and seemed to take to the sailors.

November 13th, Friday.—Until further orders we are always to have a march in the morning, which is a very good thing, as the men have but little to do just at present.

November 14th, Saturday.—Of this day the writer of this diary could find no record anywhere among the notes he put down each day on the spot, but nothing particular that he could recollect took place.

November 15th, Sunday.—This afternoon Lieutenant Hay got orders to take a few men up the river with him in a small steamer called the "Barraponta" laying here, for the purpose of seeing whether he could see any parties of the enemy anywhere on the banks of the river. He went with 26 men, but returned again this evening without any adventure.

Monday, November 16th.—We had our usual march this morning at half-past six o'clock. We found our names down in the garrison orders to-day to supply a picquet at the other side of the bridge, so Garvey and a picquet of our men went.

Tuesday, November 17th.—Our picquet returned this evening, and we are ordered to supply it again to-morrow morning, as there are so few soldiers here to take it. The engineer who is with us is to go.

Wednesday, November 18th.—We furnished the picquet accordingly to-day in charge of the engineer. We expect to hear of something curious happening during the night, as he does not know anything about what he has to do, not being in that line, but as Lieutenant Hay does not want to send either Lascelles or myself, there is no one else to go.

November 19th, Thursday.—As we expected, a most curious adventure happened last night. During the night one of our sentries on picquet, a marine, challenged a man passing and received no answer, so he blazed away at him, and the unfortunate being, a native, was found dead this morning. The engineer, for what reason we don't know, sent the body up to Lieutenant Hay's tent this morning, so the first thing he saw on waking up was, as he expressed it " black game " borne on four men's shoulders. There was an enquiry on it this morning, and it was found that the sentry did nothing more than his duty in firing. The native was a Christian, and buried this afternoon.

November 20th, Saturday.—Some more of our men went some way up the river this morning in the steamer "Barraponta," but as I went in her last time, I did not go to-day. They came back again as they could not find out anything in consequence of there not being enough water to take them up high enough.

November 22nd, Sunday.—To-day being Sunday, we marched our men to the church here, when Mr. Moore preached and had a very nice service. The actual church itself is undergoing repairs, so we had prayers in a kind of school adjoining it.

November 23rd, Monday.—We have now heard a good many particulars about the relief of Lucknow where all our fellows are. They are getting on capitally and distinguishing themselves very much. Daniels, one of our midshipmen, and one of the best fellows in our mess, has been killed and several others wounded, but we are not yet sure of their names. This morning at six o'clock, according to General Wyndham's orders, we marched our men down to the canal, and made a bridge across it with planks and native boats, for the purpose of seeing how soon we could do it in case of an emergency. It succeeded very well.

November 24th, Tuesday.—Had our usual march this morning, and during the day heard more particulars from Lucknow, viz., that one place had been stormed and taken by our fellows, and 2000 of the enemy killed in one spot, and that they are fighting their way on through the town.

November 25th, Wednesday.—During the whole time we have been here, we have been hearing rumours of a force of the enemy, called the Gwalior contingent, who are supposed to have intentions of attacking this place, and are reported each day to be advancing. They are now reported to be at a place called Calpee, which is only 16 miles away from here, so consequently all the detachments of regiments that are here and that can be spared have encamped on the Calpee road, about a mile and a half from this camp. It would be a good opportunity for them now if they really want to attack us, for almost all but a few detachments of regiments are gone on to Lucknow, and regiments that are on their way up never remain here, but go on to Lucknow immediately; but in the future I believe they are to be stopped, as we are now in such a critical position. I am getting on very comfortably at Mr. Moore's bungalow; and Dangerfield, who is staying with him, is a very jolly, good-natured fellow. There is a swimming bath about a mile away from the town, belonging to Mr. Moore, and it is attached to a house which he has bought, and intends soon to live in. We often go out there and have a bath, and the other day I was there bathing by myself, and had just got out of the water, when I heard the alarm faintly sounded, as if it was somewhere in the centre of the town. I made up my mind that we were attacked, so hurried on my clothes anyhow, and ran as hard as I could for the town, expecting every moment to get cut off, as the swimming bath was right out in the country, and quite a mile away from the town; but when I got to the bridge which led over the canal to the town, I found a party of native police riflemen practising skirmishing and bugle sounds, &c., and of course saw directly that it was them, which was a great relief for the moment, but I was sorry for it afterwards, as we are in want of some excitement, as for the time being we are leading rather a monotonous kind of life.

November 26th, Thursday.—To-day has been all excitement. A large advanced party of the enemy advanced early this morning close up to our camp, on the Calpee road. Our fellows met them and drove them back, capturing two guns. Our own sailors took no part in the action, as we were not wanted, and the heavy guns were not required. In case of our being wanted to move out of the entrenched camp, we are to have charge of two heavy siege train guns. Orders came late this evening to hold ourselves in readiness to join the camp early to-morrow morning on the Calpee road, and that an action was expected, as the party that was driven back yesterday was only a kind of advanced guard, and that the whole bulk of the Gwalior contingent was expected to come down on us to-morrow. We are all to go.

November 27th, Friday.—This morning at daybreak we were up and joined our party in the entrenched camp, who had already struck tents, and with our two 24-pounders were preparing for the march. I looked forward with great excitement and pleasure to at last being under fire, which we all had made up our minds to to-day. We soon got in motion, and as we were not in company with any other regiment or body of men, we marched off for the camp on the Calpee road, outside the town, where we arrived about seven a.m. Here we found General Wyndham and staff galloping about the camp, smoking a cigar all the while, which he is very fond of, but giving orders, &c., and getting everything prepared for action. Dangerfield has come with us as a volunteer, just to see the fun. He is an old hand at it, having been in numbers of actions with General Havelock. We halted our two guns on our arrival in the centre of the road (Grand Trunk), and the camp is pitched on both sides of it. We got our servants to work immediately, and they knocked up a hole in the ground, made a fire, and made us a kind of breakfast, very acceptable after our early march (as we thought) as we sat down on the bank at the side of the road eating it. About eleven we heard that an attack was not expected after all, as the enemy had shown no signs of advancing, so Lieutenant Hay sent Garvey back to see after our tents, which had not made their appearance yet; however, he met them about half way, and with the application of a little bamboo to the backs of the niggers driving the elephants upon which were our tents, he soon got them up to the camp, but no sooner had he arrived and was consulting with Lieutenant Hay about the position we were to encamp in, than to our surprise the alarm sounded. There was a regular hum all over the camp immediately, general assemblies sounding for the regiment to fall in, horses saddling, and officers galloping about all over the camp in a tremendous state of excitement. Our tents not being yet pitched, we were "all there" as the saying is, and had nothing to do but go at once to our two guns. But alas! the guns have no sights like guns on board ship, as they come from Cawnpore, and are meant only for artillery. Some one proposed to get some bits of wood and lash them to the guns as there is nothing better. " No sooner said than done." Some sticks of strong wood were got and cut out about the height, as far as could be guessed, and we soon had a wooden dispart lashed on. While we were thus employed, the regiments had all fallen in, and our piquets were being driven in, we could see clouds of dust as men stationed on outpost duty came galloping in as hard as they could tear, all with different yarns, especially a lot of Sowars and native cavalry, who came in with all manner of wonderful reports about the strength of the enemy, &c. We could not see far, as on both sides of the road ahead of us it was deeply wooded, with only a break here and there. Clouds of dust could now and then be seen all along the horizon, on ahead of us, and everything indicated the certain approach of an enemy, and evidently a large force. Commodore Rowley Lambert was with us, he came out as a volunteer; of course had no duty to do or anything of that kind, as he was not with us officially, but he attached himself as a looker on to us, as he belonged to the service. While we were all talking, looking at the approach of this tremendous force, as we were convinced it must be, we heard a heavy gun, then a long whiz-iz-iz like a rocket, and a shell burst. It was a beautiful day, very hot, and the sky quite blue. The shell burst very high and a long way off from where we were, and the white smoke oozing out from it against the bright blue sky looked beautiful. It was the first shell that I ever saw fired in real warfare, and I shall never forget it as long as I live. Some detachments of regiments, amongst which were some of the Rifles, got orders to move on ahead of us. We had not more than 1,500 or 2,000 men in all. Our orders soon came to move on, and to halt opposite a small ruined village containing a few huts, on the left hand side of the road. The cannonade on our retreating piquets was now much brisker, but we could not yet see anything of them. However, on halting at our appointed station, we soon saw a large gun, with a crowd of men round it, advancing along the road. They were from 800 to 1000 yards off, and appeared to halt when we did. We immediately unharnessed bullocks, unlimbered our guns, and loaded. In the meantime, orders came down for us to fire as soon as ready. We lost no time and let them have it at once. No sooner had the smoke cleared off than a kind of murmur ran round the men, "Here's one for us!" and they were not far wrong, for immediately we saw a cloud of white smoke from our adversary's gun, a bright flash, a long bang, and a long whiz-iz-iz. The shot knocked up the dust about a hundred yards ahead of us, and came tearing along at a tremendous pace right between our two guns. Luckily no one was standing in the way, or they would have been eased of their legs very quickly. We had not time to look whether it knocked over any unfortunate individual in our rear, as it was now our duty to return the compliment, which we did by firing away our two guns as hard as we could pelt, so fast indeed that it was all we could do to bring up the ammunition from the waggon in the rear. We now got it right and left, and the fire gradually increased upon us, without our scarcely noticing it, as we were so intent about keeping up our fire. We had not been long at this work, when guns opened on both flanks. We got a perfect shower of grape, which came from a gun on the right hand side of the road.

One man got hit in the leg. It made a great hole in his trousers, but as there was not much blood, and did not seem a bad wound, he managed to limp off to the rear without assistance, and bandaged up his leg. The fire was getting gradually heavier and heavier, the soldiers were skirmishing on both sides of the road, firing at the enemy whenever they got a chance, but the wood was so thick, they could seldom get a good view of them. There were some small guns placed along the left side of the road manned by Madras native artillerymen; they kept up a continuous fire. They kept it up against the enemy on the right hand side of the road, their guns being on the left side and pointed across the road, but we had nothing to keep off the fire on our left flank, which was more open, although the enemy were concealed. Their shot came bounding along at a furious rate, sometimes right over our heads, knocking down trees and cutting off branches on the other side of the road. We were in a very bad position, being just where two branch roads joined on to the " Grand Trunk " as I will try and show by this :—

Cawnpore, 27th November, 1857.

We therefore had guns firing into us on both sides as well as those ahead of us on the road, of which we could only see one. We had been going on for a long while like this, when the guns on our right annoyed us so much with their grape, that we pointed our right hand gun towards them and gave them a few rounds, but as we could not see them, it was quite guess work, and as the guns ahead immediately opened double the fire on us, so we had to right ours again. The Madras guns kept pounding away but seemingly without effect, whereas the enemy had got our exact range and position, knowing that we were on the road. General Dupuis, in command of the artillery, came and took up his station just behind our guns. The enemy were evidently advancing their guns on each side, and the fire got terrific. There was no standing this. General Dupuis, after a little hesitation, gave the order to retire a little, so as to get the guns out of their present position which it was impossible for us to hold. We immediately went for the bullocks which were on one side of the road, and hunted out the bullock-drivers who were stowed away in a ditch trembling with fright, but no sooner had we got them up than off set one of them, and all the rest followed, bullocks and all. The niggers were perfectly mad with fright. Our men rushed back and tried to stop them, officers came out with their swords, and did all in their power to stop them but it was no good. Some of the bullocks had their ears and horns cut off with the shot and were frantic with pain, and this combined with the beating and yelling of their frightened drivers made them quite dangerous to go near. Before the General had given us orders to retire, there was a slight confusion amongst the troops on either side of us. Men were getting knocked over right and left, and the fire getting fiercer every minute, but there were no orders for them either to advance or retreat out of their position. The bullocks running away increased the confusion, and a cry of "Cavalry" was raised, and an idea seemed to come over them they were being surrounded, which we certainly should have been, had we stopped there much longer. The whole force then slowly retreated. The Madras artillerymen secured two or three of their bullocks and got two or three of their guns away. Our men held on well, but were obliged to retreat with the others. As we were leaving our guns, one of our Marines got knocked over by a round shot, and the cannonade, if possible, seemed worse than ever. We had no drag-ropes, so were obliged to leave the guns. At last we caught some of the runaway bullocks, rallied some men together, and with a good many of the Rifles and other detachments advanced again. We had also a few of the native cavalry with us; we made a rush up the road again, and came up to our guns which were not yet touched by the enemy, although by their musketry we could tell they were close to us. We limbered up immediately, harnessed in the bullocks, and began moving the guns back. The fire began again worse than ever, and the troops that had pressed on were again driven back, and a general retreat began. We passed our camp on fire, we had no time to strike any tents, or save anything, so some of our men set fire to all they could. Luckily, our tents had not been pitched before the action began, and so we were allright. When we got to the town the sight was miserable. All the natives had shut their shops, and the narrow streets were cram full of guns, horses without riders, bullocks, and men, there was scarcely room to move in some places. One gun stuck in the ruins of a house and we had to leave it. When we got to the entrenched camp we found it in a dreadful state of confusion. The alarm had of course spread all over the town, and every one had come rushing in, as the entrenched camp was the great safe-guard of the town, being very strong. Here we found Mr. Moore, who had brought in most of his things, and had taken care that our servants should bring in our (Lascelles' and mine) boxes. Lieut. Hay had been wounded in two places, and was unfit for duty, so Garvey (mate) took the command of our men. Commander Rowley Lambert goodnaturedly "lending him a hand." The first thing we did was to station men to the different guns round the fort. We had a few artillerymen, and these with some sheiks and Madras men manned the rest of the guns. It soon got dark after we got in. The action lasted from half-past eleven till half-past four p.m. The excitement was so great it seemed to me scarcely an hour or so. Before dark every one was in the entrenched camp except a regiment or two who had charge of houses and buildings outside; the whole of the native part of the town we left to the enemy, as we had not enough men to defend it. In the evening I went with Mr. Moore to his house, it was quite dark and rather ticklish work, as the enemy's position was not known, but this was close to one of our piquets, and we could soon have raised the alarm with our revolvers. However we managed to get a few things Mr. Moore wanted, and got back again all safe. We stationed our men for the night at the guns, as an attack was expected every moment, and it would not be safe to go away from them. The enemy remained quite quiet all night, except now and then a little musketry between them and our men stationed outside. The gun was got back (that we left in the town) in the middle of the night. It was done quietly, and although the enemy must have been all round, being in an out of the way place, they got it back all safe.

November, 28th, Saturday.—This morning turned out dull and very hot, a dry sultry heat. About half-past five o'clock this morning I got up, having tried to get some sleep on my charpoy which I had placed outside a tent which Lieutenant Hay had pitched for him, as he had to lay up with his wound. We had to put all our traps inside the tent as it was not safe to leave them out, so there was no room for me. However I managed pretty well as I was not quite in the open air, as the top of the tent came over the side a little and I got under that. There were several alarms during the night, and we had to sleep with our clothes and boots on all ready. About 8 a.m. everyone began to wonder that the enemy had not made any attack on us, but they were soon made easy on that score, for between 9 and 10 o'clock all along the horizon to the left of the camp we saw large bodies of men approaching, kicking up a tremendous dust. The front of the camp looked over the Cantonments and Town, a few houses and buildings of which we garrisoned. On our right was the Ganges, with the bridge of boats crossing over into Oude, so that the points we expected to be attacked were our front and left flank, but nothing was apprehended on our right, as they could not cross the river without the bridge of boats which we defended, and kept a piquet of soldiers on the Oude side of it. At the same time that these bodies of men were seen on our left, we also occasionally saw some among the houses of the town, who opened musketry on our advanced positions. The rifles were soon ordered out to meet the enemy on the left: they had been stationed outside during the night. The 64th regiment, most of which had been holding positions outside the camp during the night, were ordered to meet the enemy on our front. In the meantime the enemy had posted guns in different positions about our left front, and opened a regular cannonade on us with shot and shell. The commencement caused a good deal of confusion, as the camp was so crowded and the fire very accurate. However, we soon got to work and opened fire with our guns, of which we had a good many, mounted all round the camp with embrasures and parapets. After about half-an-hour very heavy firing the enemy slackened theirs into a steady bombardment, mostly using shell. We have got a hospital inside the camp and their fire seemed chiefly directed on that. The Rifles soon met the enemy and we heard them peppering away like fun, although houses and trees hid them from view. A tremendous musketry fire soon began from where the 64th were, and numbers of them were soon brought in dreadfully wounded, and taken to the hospital. The cannonade between our guns and the enemy went on the whole morning; we could see them quite plain occasionally running across a road which went down towards the town from the gates of our camp. The Sepoys seemed all neatly dressed in red jackets and white trousers. I had some shots at some of them with a a rifle as they were running across the road. The men of the 64th regiment were being brought in by numbers, dreadfully wounded, and the hospital is already full. The enemy have got the range of it beautifully, and the shot often strikes it. About one p.m. an order came for us (the sailors) to go to the place where the Rifles were engaged, and bring in two guns which the former had captured from the enemy. We took as many men as we could spare from the guns, and Garvey and myself went with them. We had orders to be as quick as we could, so we set off running as hard as we could pelt. Unfortunately we had to carry some drag ropes to bring the guns back with, which delayed us a good deal. We had to go for some way along on our left, right away from the town till we came to a village, and there we were told the Rifles had been fighting some way the other side of it, so we cocked our revolvers and ran right through as hard as we could. When we got to the other side of it we found ourselves in a large ploughed field, but could see nothing of the Rifles whom we were in search of. However we saw some horsemen galloping across towards us as hard as they could; and the enemy, who had some guns posted at the bottom end of the field, kept up a continual fire on them, and we could see the shot knocking up the earth close to their horses. When they got nearer, we saw they were General Wyndham and his staff. The former came up to us and told us whereabouts the Rifles were, and that they had got on famously. We set off down a road to which he had directed us, and met the Rifles coming back with the

captured guns. We hooked on the drag-ropes, and the
Rifles and our men manned them. Some Rifle officers
told us they had had very hard fighting all the morning,
and that their Colonel was killed. The guns were soon
got back and we entered the entrenched camp with them
amidst tremendous cheering from us, and from all those
who had a voice to shout in the entrenched camp. Towards the evening the 64th returned, having had tremendous fighting all day. They charged the enemy's guns
and drove them away, but they got attacked by cavalry,
and after a great deal of hand to hand fighting, our men
had to fall back quite overcome by numbers. Brigadier
Little, their colonel, a major, and numbers of officers and
men were killed. They were mustered outside the
entrenched camp before they came in, and they were
scarcely half the number they went out. In the hurry of
the retreat a great deal of stores of different kinds was
left just outside the camp, belonging to private individuals;
as there was no room inside they had to remain there, and
among them were some casks of beer and wine, and some
of the soldiers found this out, and by some means got at
it, and there were a great many cases of drunkenness
among them, and the howling and noise they kept up
through the night, as they were prisoners at the main
guard, was enough to prevent anyone from sleeping, to
say nothing of the continual alarms we had throughout
the night. The sailors remained very steady, and not
one case of drunkenness occurred among them. About
every hour the enemy gave heavy rolls of musketry, which
caused the word to "Stand to your arms" to be continually
passed, but nothing came of it, except a good many musket

balls whistling about our heads, as they managed to creep up in the dark within easy musketry distance.

November 29th, Sunday.—This Sunday was rather different to quiet ones spent in England. As soon as it got daylight, the enemy began their cannonade on us, and encroached a good deal on us. After a good deal of musketry work our men had to leave some of the outer positions we had occupied, and so we held only two or three houses close outside the camp. The enemy, as the morning advanced, got very impatient, and had the impertinence of advancing a heavy gun up a road in front of us and in our full view. They fired away with great precision, and their shot came full swing into our camp, and right into the very doors of the hospital. Lascelles and I were standing behind the parapet when we saw a shot knock up the dust just into our front. We luckily bobbed our heads, and I slipped and came against Lascelles, which knocked him down on a pile of bayonets (luckily in scabbards), and we both rolled over together, much to the amusement of the bystanders; the shot just grazed the parapet where we had been looking over, and bounded on to the top of an ammunition cart just behind us, which gave it a spring, and it went right off into the middle of the camp. If this had not happened, one of us would certainly have been minus our head, as the shot passed exactly over the part of the parapet where our heads had been. This afternoon the welcome intelligence arrived of Sir Colin Campbell having encamped about 10 miles the other side of the river, and so will be here to-morrow. During the day the enemy made several attempts to set fire to the bridge of boats, which would have been a dreadful thing to us if they had succeeded, but luckily they did not. They made a kind of raft, and set it on fire, and then let it float down towards the bridge with the current, but it was destroyed before it reached it. They also kept up a tremendous fire on it (the bridge) the whole day, but without doing it any damage to signify. They kept pretty quiet during the night, occasionally a little musketry as if they had an idea of making an attack, but nothing came of it.

November 30th, Monday.—The enemy again commenced their cannonade on us the first thing this morning, but Sir Colin pushed on two of his Naval Brigade guns from his force before the others, to the banks of the river, on the Oude side, and they began firing on the town, which was a good thing for us, and damped the enemy's fire considerably. About nine a.m. Sir Colin Campbell's force arrived, and began crossing over the bridge, and a very welcome sight they presented, for we could not have held out much longer, shut up as we were with our small force. Captain Peel came up to see us and seemed very jolly, and pleased with the men whom he said had behaved splendidly at Lucknow. He seemed to think a good deal of Lieut. Hay's wound. He was hit in the stomach on the day of our retreat by a grape shot, which was almost spent, and may have done him a good deal of internal injury. Lieut. Salmon, one of our mess, has been wounded at Lucknow, he was shot through the thigh, and as he is doing well and got recommended for the Victoria Cross, he is a lucky fellow. They were close up to a wall from which the Sepoys were throwing hand gunades, one man especially doing a great deal of damage, and Captain Peel called out that whoever would jump up into a tree that was close by, and shoot that man, he would recommend him for the Victoria Cross. Lieut. Salmon was up in a minute, shot the man, and in the meantime got wounded. Captain Peel consequently recommended him, also Lieut. Young for bringing up some guns within a few yards of a building crowded with the enemy, and with two or three hands working and firing the guns. I went down to the river side, where our guns were with Captain Peel, and saw all our fellows, and among them Mr. Bowman, our old tent mate; they all seemed very jolly, but rather suprised at finding us fighting at Cawnpore, when they had only just left it at Lucknow. Sir Colin's army form an immense long line; they have also all the women and children with them that they rescued out of the Residency. The force is to encamp some way to the left of the entrenchment camp, on some open ground, upon which the enemy have not yet encroached, but which is facing them and the town. There are a few buildings in the rear of the camp, in which the women and children are to be put until they can be conveyed down the country. Lascelles and myself got orders from the Captain to join his part of the brigade, and to resume duties as his aides-de-camp, so we got our baggage out of the entrenched camp, and joined their encampment, leaving Garvey and the 50 men in the entrenched camp. We soon got our tent pitched, having Mr. Bowman as tent mate the same as before, and had lots to tell about our proceedings at Cawnpore, and Mr. Bowman about Lucknow. The enemy soon found out where we had encamped and gave a shot now and then, but seemed quite dismayed (if we could judge from their fire) at the strength of our reinforcements from Lucknow. The only part they kept a heavy fire upon was the bridge, as it was so crowded with men, women, camels, bullocks, horses, elephants, carts, mules, and all the appendages of a large army. Occasionally, if a shot came into the middle of them, it made a good deal of damage and confusion, but their shot generally passed over their heads and hit the water the other side, but before night every one had passed over. There are a great many sick and wounded officers with them, some of whom have been in the residency all the while, but they will all have plenty of opportunities of going down the country, as numbers of escorts are going down with the women and children. The enemy still keep up a heavy fire on the entrenched camp, and it is quite a relief to be out of it. Our two guns were withdrawn this evening from the river side.

December 1st, Tuesday.—The enemy's guns began again this morning, and ours from the entrenched camp return the compliment very briskly. About half-past ten this morning, a gun, which the enemy had posted somewhere near the centre of the town, opened fire on our camp, and got the range so exactly, that the first shot they fired struck the ground by some ammunition carts just in front of us, and went right into a tent in our rear, and wounded a sergeant of artillery. The second shot they fired went close to our tent, and went right through the body of Mr. Bowman's syce, who was grooming his pony behind his tent. Another shell they fired burst in one of the tents of the 93rd Highlanders, and killed three of them. An aide-de-camp soon came galloping up to Capt. Peel's tent, and he immediately gave orders for us to fall in, and get ready for action. One of our heavy 24 pounders, and our two 8-inch howitzers were sent to a battery on the right of the camp, which our men made up with sand bags, and commanded a splendid view of the town and enemy. Lieut. Vaughan, our 1st Lieut, took charge of it; and it was afterwards given to Kerr, one of our senior midshipmen. Captain Peel, with the rest of us, and some guns and rockets went into the town, to see, if with the assistance of some regiments, we could not force the enemy back across the canal, which runs right through the town. We soon got among them, as we went right up a street, both sides of which were crowded with native houses and huts, which a few yards further on, we could see were crowded with the enemy, who were firing away at us like fun, but as they did not dare to show themselves much, they could not do us much harm. We halted one gun at the corner of the street, and Captain Peel, with Lieut. Young, Lascelles, and myself, with two rockets, and men, went in among some houses to the right of the street, where we found a nice little square place surrounded by huts, where we placed our two rockets. We saw from the smoke where the enemy were, and fired a rocket right into the middle of them. This seemed to surprise them very much, and their musketry slackened for a minute or so, but not for long, as they had seen where our rocket came from, and down came a tremendous shower of bullets, quite like a storm of hail; luckily there was a kind of shed place which was roofed, and we got under it for the time, the bullets whistling past and spattering down over our heads. Every now and then two or three of us jumped out and fired one of the rockets and then popped into our shed again, however we fired the rockets so fast at last that they did not seem at all to appreciate it and their fire slackened very much. While all this is going on we never see anything at all of the native inhabitants of the town, most of them burying themselves in holes under ground with their treasure, and except for us and the Sepoys the town every where appears quite deserted. Our Marines who ought to have come with our party into the Town misunderstood the Captain's orders and went off to the battery where our other guns were some way off, so Captin Peel sent me to tell them to join us, I had a long hunt after them as I did not exactly know the position of the battery, and had to go across an open plain where I was warmly saluted with sundry musket balls; I found them at last (the Marines) and in marching back across the plain their red coats made such a good target we got peppered at tremendously. When I got back to our party I found they had moved a 24-pounder up the street and were trying to silence an enemy's gun that had been playing on them from the other end of the street. The marines immediately began picking the Sepoys off who were standing round their gun, and we fired away as fast as we could load. About the 4th shot after I had come back struck the carriage of their gun, and quite silenced it and they all seemed to have left it, however thy kept up a tremendous fire of musketry from both sides of the street, the sheiks (a regiment of them) were with us acting as a cover to our guns, and 12 of them were killed and wounded. One of our blue jackets was standing with two others in the rear of our gun when a round shot came, killed him, and wounded two others so dangerously that they will both have their legs amputated and then will not be expected to live. One of our marines got also very badly wounded in the foot by a musket ball. We were in great hopes of capturing this gun of the enemy's, but as they did not dare expose themselves to our fire they had a rope made fast to the gun and pulled it away in at the side of the street where they were concealed, without exposing themselves in the least. Two or three more of the enemy's guns opened on us soon after this and kept up a lively fire. The 8th Regiment were acting as a kind of reserve, and their Officers had some "tiffin" brought down from the camp, and asked us to have some with them so I made an ample repast. They established themselves behind a wall, and most of the shot went over our heads. We kept up a kind of desultory fire with the enemy all the afternoon, but as we could not do much we got orders to withdraw the guns before dusk, and went back to camp. The enemy have been pounding away at the entrenched camp all the day. One of the two men who were wounded died, the other had his leg amputated, but is likely to live.

December 2nd, Wednesday.—We always have parade very regularly every morning, when we are not away from our camp on duty. The usual routine is for the men to fall in, arms to be inspected and then when that is done the band which always plays while this is going on, goes to the rear, a general salute is given, and the band plays the National Anthem; Captin Peel always acknowledges the salute. After this the drill begins which generally lasts from half-an-hour to an hour, and ends by marching round a square in sections and sub-divisions, the band playing in the centre. Numbers of soldiers come to see our parades, and are very much pleased with the good marching and order of the men. The enemy were moderately quiet all to-day, our batteries of which we have two now, have had a good deal of work, but we have not all been called out for anything. In the night the enemy attacked our camp, but made the attack some way from us, so our guns were not wanted, and they were soon driven away by the 88th and 53rd regiments. It was more a reconnoitring expedition on their part than anything else, as they did not come out in much force.

December 3rd, Thursday.—Just as we dismissed from our parade this morning, some guns opened fire on our camp, and as they have the right range the shot went plump in among our tents. It is most provoking our camp being pitched within reach of their fire, as there is more space that would do for camp ground in our rear. However, one of our 24-pounders from Lieut. Vaughan's battery, hit, or seemed to hit, the exact spot they were firing from (as we could not see the gun because of the houses and huts among which it was hid) and quite silenced it for a time. The women and children with all their appendages are being sent down the country to Allahabad daily under strong escorts; it is supposed that we shall not make any decisive attack on the enemy until we are quite clear of them. Captain Peel sent me on a message, after dark, to Lieut. Vaughan's battery, but it was so dark that I could not find him, but came upon the house for the Commander-in-Chief of the station, which had been entrenched and made a hospital of while we were shut up in the entrenched camp. In one of the rooms

I found General Wyndham with his aides-de-camp and a lot of other officers, the general helped me out of my difficulty by showing me the direction to go, and how to keep out from getting among the enemy, as it was quite dark. A captain of the 88th said he would walk up with me, as he wanted to reconnoitre the ground about where we had to go, and I found the battery all right. Soon after I got back to our camp we were all turned out, and the guns got ready with the bullocks, as an attack on our part of the camp was expected, so we had all to sleep with our clothes on, and by our arms, but nothing happened.

December 4th, Friday.—The enemy have been much quieter all to-day, occasionally shots were exchanged between them and our batteries, and occasionally a good many sharp rolls of musketry, but they are reported to be crossing over the Ganges into Oude, most likely intending to attack our right flank from the other side of the river. They can only be crossing over, if they are doing so, by very small detachments, as the town is full of them, and they seem daily to be receiving reinforcements. Every now and then we catch sight of lots of cavalry, and also horse artillery, which nobody expected they would have, as they had very little of the latter when they were in our service. Cavalry of course they always had plenty of.

December 5th, Saturday.—The enemy made several vain attempts to-day to set fire to the bridge of boats, but it was no use. However, they kept up a tremendous cannonade on it, and several shots went right through the picquet tent on the other side of the river. There are rumours going about the camp to-day that the grand attack on the enemy is to be made to-morrow, as all the rescued women and children have now gone down the country. As the enemy have got so well established, and reinforced in the town, it is expected that there will be a hard fight. The Nana is reported to have taken command of them, and two officers, one of the 64th, that were taken prisoners the day of the retreat, are said to have been beaten to death by slippers; a favourite punishment of theirs.

December 6th, Sunday.—This morning about half-past six, orders came to strike tents, get everything ready for action, and await orders. There was a great excitement among us all, especially when we heard it was for the grand attack. About 8 o'clock, we being all ready, we got orders to move on towards the left of the camp, and halted the guns some way on our left on a road, and quite on the left of the town. We halted behind some buildings in the suburbs of the town, and to the left of them there was a large open plain stretching right out into the country, the town being on the right. After halting our guns, the regiments that were selected for the attack began to fall in on our rear. They were all Sir Colin's force except some who were with General Mansfield and the party in the entrenched camp, who were to attack the enemy in the centre of the town. Among our force we had the 93rd Highlanders, and 42nd Highlanders, who arrived from Allahabad about half-an-hour before the action began. The 42nd Highlanders was the regiment that just joined us; the 93rd were with us through all the operations at Cawnpore; the 93rd were at Lucknow, and a famous regiment. We also had the 53rd and 23rd regiments. After they had all arrived we got orders to advance and continued our course on the road going towards our left, and in front of the open plain. Our guns took the lead of all, consisting of three 24-pounders, one 8-inch howitzer, and two rocket tubes. Then followed two heavy guns manned by Royal Artillerymen, and the army in the rear. We advanced along the road a little way which led us right out into the open. Across the plain, quite on the other side of it, the enemy were in force among some jungle, and had several guns. They were close to the canal, across which a bridge runs, and on this bridge they had posted two heavy guns. They allowed us to go on quite unmolested, and did not even seem to have perceived us at all. As soon as we got well into the open we branched off from the road, and went down the plain towards the enemy. We got within 800 yards of them, and then unlimbered the guns and opened fire. The enemy seemed entirely taken by surprise, and were very slow in answering; however, when they did they fired with great precision. They had again in this instance the advantage of being partly concealed among wood and jungle, while we were in a perfectly open space, and offered them a good target. The Marines and the 53rd regiment acted as a covering party to our guns, and behaved splendidly, skirmishing all round us. The rest of the force were drawn up two deep in a long line, a few hundred yards in our rear, and advanced in beautiful line, quite as if they were moved along in a straight line by machinery. After firing at each other for some time, we began advancing the guns one by one, keeping with the front line of skirmishers all the while. As we began advancing, there was a kind of rush forward among the enemy; and Captain Peel said afterwards that he had made up his mind they would charge the guns, but they fell back again, and there seemed to be a great deal of confusion among them, as if they were quite surprised at heavy guns coming along taking the lead like ours did. Our men manned the drag-ropes and pulled the guns on by them, if we had but a short distance to advance; and if it was some way we harnessed in the bullocks, who were always kept handy, much to the disgust of the native bullock drivers, who did not like it at all, but on the whole they did their work well, no doubt they saw they were likely to get the best of it, and had an eye to the loot they might get if we were successful. We got very close to them in this way, advancing one gun after another, and we got the guns on the road which went across the canal by the bridge, so that we were exactly in front of the two guns we had posted there, and they fired at us point blank, grape and cannister as we came up the road. The fire got very hot indeed, two of our men were wounded, two or three of the sheiks who had also been sent to help to cover up the guns were wounded close to us. One man I saw killed, very close to me, by a bit of shell, and every now and then on looking round, I could see great gaps made in the long line of soldiers in our rear by the shot. However Captain Peel led the way, and our men got on the guns, and began cheering as they advanced. The Marines and 53rd regiment on both sides of us, were making good use of their time, and keeping up a tremendous fire of musketry among the hillocks and uneven ground on each side of the road. We persisted in our advance, and the enemy could stand it no longer,

but fairly ran. Occasionally same of them faced round
and gave us a volley of musketry, which came whizzing
and spattering round us, and then turned round again.
On seeing them run, the whole force set up a tremendous
cheer, and all the soldiers, Highlanders, and all, were
ordered to "double," and soon came up with us, some of
them lending our men a hand at the drag-ropes, as we
kept on dragging some of the guns, in case the enemy
were to make a stand, and the guns should be wanted in
a hurry, and we did not harness in the bullocks till afterwards. We pursued them for about 8 miles on the Calpee
road. As we went along, about every 50 yards, we came
across heaps of the enemy lying across the road, with
large cuts and gashes which they had received from our
cavalry. Sir Colin went on with the 9th Lancers about
five miles further than the place we halted at, but they
could not do much as the ground was very uneven, and the
enemy disappeared so wonderfully quick. We waited till
Sir Colin came back, and then had orders to march back,
and we encamped about a mile from Cawnpore. The road
was covered with ammunition, &c., which we could not
take away, so we blew it all up. We did not get to our
camping ground till quite late, and we were all tired and
glad to get some rest. We could not pitch tents as the
baggage had remained behind at Cawnpore, so we could
only sleep under guns and put up in the best places we could.
Clinton, 1st Lieut, and myself, slept under a captured gun,
one of the 17 that we had taken from the enemy that day.
After the enemy had commenced to retreat, and while our
cavalry were pushing forward, an officer and a private of
the 9th Lancers, as they were galloping across a field, fell,

horses and all, into a well; the grass had grown up all round the sides of it, and what with the dust and excitement they could not see it. We were passing by this well when we saw some soldiers looking down, and Captain Peel went up and found out what had happened, so we got some of our men together, and Captain Peel directing them, they were both landed up all safe by some drag-ropes belonging to our guns. The horses were both lost, and both officer and man were in a very exhausted state, the former had kept hold of his sword all the while in his hand. They said they had given up all hopes of being saved, as the horses had got very restless in the water, and they could hardly keep them under.

December 7th, Monday.—Our tents and baggage arrived early this morning, and the former were soon pitched, although in a bad camp ground, as it was a sandy plain. A pursuing column was sent on toward Calpee, under command of General Grant. Nothing was done otherwise to-day, and it was entirely given up to the men to rest after their exertions of the day before. General Mansfield was quite successful in his attack on the enemy in the centre of the town, and drove them all out of it; so now Cawnpore is quite clear of them. The natives are now coming out by degrees from their holes and hiding places under ground, where they have been hidden during all the fighting. Among some of these natives who came out from the town, was a native servant, whom I had discharged just after our troops had re-taken Cawnpore, and he had come out of his hiding place, he met an officer and a party of men coming down a street, and as he was tall and had moustaches, he had every appearance of a Sepoy, and this officer accused him of being one, and he was going to be shot at once only he hunted out the certificate which I had given him on leaving, and that just saved him in time.

December 8th, Tuesday.—To-day, after our parade, a man was flogged for theft. He stole some money belonging to one of our officers. This is the first case of flogging a blue jacket since the "Shannon" has been commissioned. In the afternoon an order came from the Commander-in-Chief for the whole camp to muster every half-hour, as some men, belonging to different regiments, had strayed away, and illused and plundered some natives.

December 9th, Wednesday.—On parade, Captain Peel gave the men a short speech, in which he told them that the Commander-in-Chief had been much pleased with them on the 6th, and that General Grant had come up with the enemy, cut some more of them up, and captured 15 more guns. We hear that we are likely to stop here for some time, and probably our next move will be further to the north. On the 6th, as we captured the whole of the enemy's camp, there has been a great deal of loot taken, especially among the sheiks, who are great hands at that kind of thing.

December 10th, Thursday.—Some printed copies of the Commander-in-Chief's despatches relating to the 6th of this month have come out, and have been sent round the men. The Naval Brigade are mentioned very handsomely, and Captain Peel, and Lieut. Vaughan especially. Our men have several times been mentioned in despatches. At the Relief of Lucknow Sir Colin says, in giving an account of the way the guns were brought up within a few yards of a building filled with the enemy, "that the withering fire of the Highlanders effectually covered the Naval Brigade from great loss, but it was an action unparalleled in warfare." At the Relief of Lucknow, besides Lieut. Salmon being wounded, we had several officers hit, and more or less hurt; but luckily escaped the fate of poor Daniels who was killed. Lieuts. Salmon and Hay, the latter still suffering from his wound got at the day of our retreat from Cawnpore, have both been sent down the country to Allahabad, but they expect soon to be able to join us again.

December 11th, Friday.—The first company, under command of Lieut. Wilson, whom we left at Allahabad, are expected to join us again soon. Some few of them ran away from their quarters, and came up the grand trunk road by attaching themselves to different detachments on their way up, and presented themselves in one camp, but they were immediately taken prisoners, and are to be sent down again to Allahabad, at which they are much disgusted as they had an idea that the Captain would admire their zeal and allow them to remain with him; but they were much mistaken.

December 12th, Saturday.—This afternoon Lieutenant Wilson and Verney (mate), arrived with 90 men of the 1st Company, and our band, which is a great acquisition. Lieut. Wratislaw is on his way up with the rest of the company.

December 13th, Sunday.—After our parade to-day we had Divine Service. The way it is done is to form a square, Mr. Bowman standing in the centre and reading the service, and in this way the whole army hears Divine Service every Sunday; each regiment forming a square round its own chaplain.

December 14th, Monday.—After parade we struck tents and moved our camp to a much nicer encampment, although within a little longer distance from Cawnpore. Captain Peel always rides a grey Arab horse, which he got at Allahabad, and a good many of our officers have got ponies and horses; I am looking out for one, but have not been able to find a both good and cheap one yet; there are numbers knocking about which the men have looted from the enemy, but they are most of them wretched animals. There are numbers of miserable ponies about the camp who are called "tats," and the natives generally use them for carrying bundles of hay, and things of that kind, which wear the skin quite off their backs, and they present a most miserable appearance. Some "knowing" natives sometimes give these ponies as much sugar-cane as they can eat for two or three days, which for the time makes them look quite sleek and fat outside, and then offer them for sale, but before the buyer has had the pony in his possession a couple of days the pony gets thin and good for nothing, and he finds out his mistake.

December 15th, Tuesday.—We had a good deal of drill to-day with our parade, going through evolutions in marching, &c. Lieutenant Vaughan had a particular knack of drilling the 1st company, for since he has been away they have rather fallen off in their drill. Lieutenant Matislaw has joined with the rest, so we are altogether now, numbering 25 officers and 560 men on parade.

December 16th, Wednesday.—We remained quite quiet to-day, except our two parades, morning and evening, which is the regular routine. Being in camp for a good many days at one place would be very monotonous, only we have so many amusements in the way of riding, &c., which I have a good deal of, and though I have not yet an animal of my own, I can always get one lent me. Mr. Bowman is a great shooter, and I often go out with him, and take long excursions into the country, although it is not always very safe, as there are lots of Sepoys and suspicious characters knocking about. Mr. Bowman always brings back plenty of game, which is a very good thing for me, being in his tent. Peacocks are plentiful, and excellent eating, quite like turkeys.

December 17th, Thursday.—The 93rd Highlanders have left our camp for a time, and encamped near Bithoor, at which place was one of Nana Sahib's chief palaces, but which is now almost entirely destroyed.

December 18th, Friday.—To-day Lieut. Vaughan, with Kerr, and an engineer, and half-a-dozen men went to Bithoor to try and recover some treasure which had been thrown down a well in that neighbourhood when the Nana evacuated the place. A chain has been made with several different parts, with hooks on the ends of them, and by means of these the Captain thinks that some of the treasure might be got up.

December 19th, Saturday.—The party that went to Bithoor returned in the evening unsuccessful, as they could get nothing. There is no doubt that, with some trouble a good deal of it could be got up, but it would be a long process.

December 20th, Sunday.—After parade we had church this morning as usual. Rumours are afloat regarding our departure, and it is said that our next move will be towards Soorutgurh which is a large town, strongly fortified by the enemy, and about 80 miles off from where we are. A great murder of Europeans took place there at the breaking out of the mutiny.

December 21st, Monday.—Our routine was altered to-day, and we had drill at 7 o'clock this morning, and our usual parade at 10 a.m. Spies are continually being caught in our camp, and our sailors have occasionally found out some of them, although a good many are brought up on suspicion, even if they had only been examining our guns and something of that kind, but they are always tried in a sort of way, and if they are innocent never get anything done to them. One of our men traced a native right round the camp, and watched and dodged him wherever he went, and as his movements gave him suspicions, he collared him, and the man was proved to be a Sepoy by a magistrate, some of whom are encamped with us.

December 22nd, Tuesday.—Nothing occurred during the day worthy of notice. A good many horses and ponies are going about among the men for sale, but I have not yet made a choice of one, as to get both a cheap and good animal is a hard thing. Our band is a great amusement in the evening, although it is not so large, or so noisy as a regimental one. Our band-master is a good one, and they play good music, which attracts a good many of both sailors and soldiers round it. They always play a little way outside our tent doors.

December 23rd, Wednesday.— This afternoon we marched out for exercise, and halted in a plain where we drilled and practised skirmishing. To-night, to our great disappointment, we found in the Commander-in-Chief's orders, which come round every night, that we are to march to-morrow. We had settled to pitch two large tents together, and give a grand dinner on Christmas Day, and ask the Captain, and make a regular day of it; but this order throws us all aback. Some felt slightly disposed to a little grumbling, but the chance of more work at Soorutgurh, to which place we are to march, kept all our spirits up. The enemy are reported to be very strongly fortified there, and we expect some more tough work.

December 24th, Thursday.—This morning at six o'clock, we struck tents and set off again on the Grand Trunk Road. The noise going on when you are woke up in the morning of a march is most confusing. What with tent pegs being knocked out, camels grunting out their most wretched dismal sounds, something between a rattle, a moan, and a grunt, elephants trumpeting, cavalry turning out and saddling, horses galloping about, bullocks being harnessed in the guns, and the shouts and yells of their drivers; then if I dont look sharp and get up, and if my tent mates (Lascelles and Mr. Bowman) happen to be very active, down comes the tent about one's ears, and one has to bundle out, yourself and posessions the best way you can. Then sometimes if your camel happens to be over-loaded he soon lets you know it, either by refusing to get up, or by capsizing everything off his back as soon as he is up. As soon as they begin to strike tents, Lascelles and I always have to go and attend on the Captain, so the servants pack the camels under Mr. Bowman's superintendence, and often if I have to come back to our tent for anything, or pass it on a message, I see him belabouring the niggers with a stick, and all our baggage in beautiful confusion on the ground. We got to the end of our march after several halts at intervals, at about half-past one p m., having marched 13 miles. The men having been encamped for so long, were rather knocked up, so the captain intends to have more marching exercise when we are next encamped for any length of time, as it is quite impossible to keep the men in training without it.

December 25th, Friday.—After parade to-day we had church, being Christmas day. At 12 o'clock our petty officers, with the band, and some of our men, marched round our tents with some large looted flags, &c., and made as much a day of it as they could, and had a double allowance of grog, commonly called on board "splicing the main brace." In the evening our tent dined with Lieut. Young's, and we had a very good cosy little Christmas dinner. The captain had asked us to dine with him, but Sir Colin had pressed him so much to go with him that he could not refuse. The captain's steward made us a very smart plum pudding, and Lieut. Young's servant, a native named Tippoo, made one against him, and I think his was the best. Some of these natives are excellent cooks, and it is quite wonderful how they do it considering the materials they have. As soon as tents are pitched, they simply grub a hole in the ground, light a fire, and put the caldron, or whatever it may be, over it, and work away, sitting all the while on their haunches, or with their legs akimbo. They are most disagreeably particular though about their own meals, and scoop out a place all round their fire where their currie is cooking, and if any European trespasses within that circle, they let out at you with all the terms of hatred and abuse they know, and then throw away their dinner, or else give it to the sweeper or parrier dog.

December 26th, Saturday.—Started again this morning at six a.m., and encamped about half-past twelve near a place called Poora. A certain number of men always go ahead under an escort before the whole force march, so as to arrive at the next encampment first, and there under the superintendence of the Quartermaster General, they mark out the different encampments, and the lines in which they are to be formed, by small flags. We (Naval Brigade) have always these flags to mark out our tents.

December 27th, Sunday.—We struck tents and marched again this morning at six o'clock, and encamped again about one p.m. after a 15 miles march. Our tents are pitched under some trees, and quite shaded by them. We hear that we are to remain here for two or three days.

December 28th, Monday.—This morning Lieutenant Young, with one of our midshipmen and a howitzer (8-inch) with a few men, joined a force under General Wyndham, and marched for a village about 8 miles off which is supposed to be in a state of mutiny, and crowded with natives, who have all been assisting the enemy, who are reported to be in force in a fort close to them. At 7 a.m. we struck tents and marched again, and encamped after going 9 miles.

December 29th, Tuesday.—This afternoon General Wyndham returned with his force. Our portion of the expedition under Lieutenant Young also returned to camp. They had a regular shooting and hanging expedition, which they described as very good fun, but they met with no resistance. They hung the chief of the village, who had assisted the enemy a great deal, and also despatched a good many other fellows in the same way. The fort they blew up, having found it deserted by the enemy. They must have gained intelligence of our sending out a force against them, as they hardly left anything behind them.

December 30th, Wednesday.—After drill and parade this morning the 93rd and 42nd Highlanders, and 53rd Regiment under command of Brigadier Hope (who had left us at Cawnpore and gone to Bithoor) arrived and joined us again. About two p.m. we heard some very heavy firing in the Soorutghurh direction, and the report is that the enemy have advanced in large forces from Soorutghurh, and marched to a bridge which they command with their guns, and now are practising their range on it. The bridge is about 15 miles from where we are encamped.

December 31st, Thursday.—We struck tents, and marched at six o'clock this morning, and encamped again about two o'clock after 12 miles march, which brings us between two or three miles of the bridge, but we have heard no firing to-day.

January 1st, 1858, Friday.—Reconnoitring parties having been sent out ahead, the bridge was found out to be broken, and part of it so much destroyed that without a great deal of work we should not be able to cross over; so after parade to-day several detachments of regiments, with a party of our men with two of our heavy guns, and an 8-inch howitzer under command of Lieutenant Vaughan were ordered to march to the bridge to protect it while being repaired.

January 2nd, Saturday.—At eight o'clock this morning

we were all thrown into a state of excitement by hearing a tremendous cannonade from the direction of the bridge. At about half-past nine we got orders to strike tents, a great relief to us, as we were very impatient to know what was going on. The nearer we got to the bridge the louder grew the firing, and we marched on a tremendous pace, our band playing all the while. The bridge was across a river named Kala Nudda, which ran at the foot of a deep valley, and surrounded on both sides by high hills. As it was only three or four miles off from where we encamped we were not long getting to the foot of the hill from the top of which the valley and bridge could be seen. On marching up this hill we were saluted by a few spent, or almost spent shot, which came rolling down occasionally. On getting to the top of the hill we found that Lieutenant Vaughan, with his party and guns, had already crossed the bridge, (which had been repaired during the night) and was peppering away at a village on the other side, which was crowded with the enemy. I went over the other side where they were, with the captain, and as we found the fire very warm, we soon had some more guns across. There were three small houses where we were, which were kept crowded with soldiers, who kept up a heavy fire of musketry. The enemy seemed to be in immense numbers, and the firing from their guns was very accurate, and came whizzing round us most unpleasantly close, but this was nothing more than we expected, as we knew they had been practising the range. The road went on from the bridge straight through the village where the enemy were, so that we could see them quite plainly. At first they kept throwing out large bodies of skirmishers along the road, and encroached so close on us that some of the 53rd were ordered out on each side of the road to keep them at bay. We had also one of our large guns brought down on the road itself, which soon made them keep close in among the houses in the village. After keeping up a cannonade on them for about two hours, Sir Colin Campbell, who was standing near our guns almost all the while, told the Captain to move one of our guns about 800 yards on our left, and advance closer to the enemy, which we did, but not without the enemy observing it, who opened on us immediataly from another gun with grape. The 8th regiment and 53rd were sent with us as a support, and they kept skirmishing all round us, and as the field was full of "doll" (a peculiar kind of weed which grows in India, and is used for food for horses, &c.) and high grass, the enemy could'nt see much of them. After we had been in the position for some time, the Captain ordered Lieutenant Lind to take a few of our men with him, and see how near he could encroach on this gun of the enemy's by skirmishing among this doll. Just before Sir Colin ordered our gun to take up the position on our left, a spent musket ball hit him in front hard enough to turn him right round, but did him no harm. Lieutenant Lind, who had advanced with his party a good way in advance, kept up a very effective fire on the enemy, who were standing round their gun, and they visibly slackened their fire. At last one well directed shot from our gun, which was pointed by Lieutenant Vaughan, knocked the gun clean out of its carriage, which was saluted by a tremendous cheer from all of us. Another shot was fired with very good direction, and the third blew up the tumbril, setting fire to all their ammunition, and blowing up a house close by, which seemed also to have been full of ammunition. We kept up a heavy fire on the village for some time longer, when scarcely any of the enemy were to be seen, and all their guns silenced. The 53rd regiment then all rose with a shout and charged the village, but without any orders to advance, and although Sir Colin Campbell and his staff immediately dashed to the front and tried to stop them, it was no good, as their voices were immediately drowned by the cheer of the regiment. The fact was that the 53rd had heard that the 93rd Highlanders had been selected for the storming party, whereat they got very indignant, as the 93rd had been kept as a reserve during the day, and had not been under fire all the while like the 53rd had, so they made up their minds to storm of their own accord. For this reason Sir Colin decided on not making out any despatches for this action, and so very few people heard of it. As there was no stopping the 53rd for the time being, the advance became general; the cavalry galloping on ahead, and mostly composed of Sheiks. The latter soon came up with the enemy, who were in full retreat and just coming out the other side of the village, and succeeded in killing 300 of them, chasing them across the fields. One or two made a stout resistance, but the greater part of them were completely panic struck, and tried to hide themselves in the ditches and grass. They left seven guns behind them, and among them were two 24-pounders, and one 18-pounder, both of them painted in a most fantastic way, with stripes round them of all the colours of the rainbow.

The others were curious looking clumsy concerns, and native made. We passed through the village, and encamped the other side of it, and about 12 miles from Suttyhur, which we were to attack next day. We got our tents by the elephants pretty soon, taking all things into consideration, but our baggage did not come till much later, and we had to content ourselves by lying down in our tents with bullock rugs or anything we could get over us till all our baggage came. The cavalry returned soon, as after getting hold of these 300 they did not go on any further, as the enemy had straggled so far all over the country, it would have been hopeless going after any more of them.

January 3rd, Sunday.—We did not strike tents till eleven o'clock this morning, as the baggage, &c., had scarcely got up to the camping ground when it broke daylight, and in consequence of the crush on the bridge, which was so crowded. We marched on towards Suttyhur, passing the 300 dead bodies which lay in the fields all along the road itself. They most of them had tremendous gashes which they had received from the Sheiks. The nearer we approached the greater grew the excitement, as we fully expected to meet with a stout resistance from the town of Soorntghurh, and we were expecting every minute to be attacked by a party sent out against us from the town, but there were no signs of the enemy anywhere. Just as we were looking out to get a sight of the town, some baboos, dressed out very swell and riding, brought us news that the town had been entirely deserted, except a few, and that they had gone during the night, and crossed the river over to the Oude side. We found on entering the town that it was exactly as the natives had described, and that not a Sepoy was to be seen, but only natives, who were all very humble, and pretended to be very glad to see us, offering milk and fruit, &c., to us as we passed through. The Commander-in-chief however got intelligence that there were still 30 Sepoys under command of a Rajah still concealed in the town, so he instantly issued a proclamation to the inhabitants that if these men were not instantly given up, he should commence bombarding the town at eight o'clock the next morning. We encamped on the parade ground, a very large one, and close to a church, which has been a very pretty one once, but was almost entirely destroyed when the Sepoys first broke out. I went in to see it, and over a door there was a marble slab pitted all over with marks from musket bullets. The Rajah with his men were brought in this evening; the latter were soon despatched, and the former kept to be hung soon.

January 4th, Monday.—Yesterday on our arrival, the fort here which is a very large strong one, was found to have been only just deserted, and one 10-inch howitzer was found loaded up to the muzzle with grape at one of the entrances. The Rajah who commanded the party of 30 Sepoys who remained in the town, was hung this evening. He was one of the Nawab of Surruckabad's leading men, and had a share in the massacre of Europeans, when the native regiments first broke out at this place.

January 5th, Tuesday.—We occasionally ride into the fort at Soorutghurh with Captain Peel, who is having some carriages made for our 8-inch ship guns that were left at

Allahabad; two of the carriages are to be made from those belonging to the 24-pounders that we captured. The fort contains an immense timber store full of wood, made, and and cut up for gun carriages, &c., and it is a wonderful thing that the enemy did not set fire to any of it, as a single match might very likely have set the whole thing on a blaze, but it is supposed that they were in too great a hurry to evacuate the place to think of it.

January 6th, Wednesday.—After our parade and drill this morning we buried one of our Marines, who died yesterday from dysentery. The grave was dug close to the church, and the whole brigade were marched up to the burial place. Lieutenant Young started in company with a force under Brigadier Hope in charge of our 24-pounders and 30 men, for a place called Mhow, where some of the enemy are reputed to be in force.

January 7th, Thursday.—Our usual drill and parade to-day, but quite quiet and no news of a move. A case of thieving has occurred among the 1st Company, who are composed of merchant seamen, who were last brought up from Calcutta. Captain Peel spoke to them about it, and gave them such a warning that the offence is not likely to be repeated, although the thief cannot be found out; this is the first grave offence that has been committed since the brigade left the ship, and this was not among the regular men-of-war's-men.

January 8th, Friday.—This afternoon we marched out of the camp for exercise, and exercised skirmishing in a large open plain. We have kept a drill sergeant belonging to the 78th Highlanders, who was engaged at Calcutta, for the purpose of assisting in the drill of the 1st Company on their way up from the river. He is a very good man, and well up in all the drills, &c.

January 9th, Saturday.—This afternoon we exercised at mounting and dismounting our 24-pounders in and out of their carriages. There was good deal of lashing, and cross lashing, and sailoring about it, which attracted a good many soldiers. It is a great thing having different ways of employing the men when idle in camp for a long while, and Captain Peel always finds numbers of ways of doing this.

January 10th, Sunday.—At eight a.m. we mustered by companies, and the Captain went round and inspected the men, after which we had church, and the 9th Lancers and Royal Artillery, having no chaplain, joined us.

January 11th, Monday.—Had a march out again this afternoon, and exercised skirmishing. The men do not dislike this at all, and rather enjoy it than otherwise. I have bought a pony, a very fair one, from a man of the 9th Lancers, who looted it from the enemy. We have great fun now and then riding about together all over the country. I was riding one afternoon with one of our Marine officers (Sterling), and we saw an officer riding down the road towards us, but by himself, so we had no idea he was any great swell, but just as he got close up to us we recognised the features of Sir Colin Campbell, and were just in time to touch our caps.

January 12th, Tuesday.—This morning Lieutenant Young and party came back from Mhow, after a rather uninteresting expedition, as they did not come in contact with the enemy at all but only had to hang a few of them.

January 13th, Wednesday.—This afternoon Lieutenant

Hay left the camp with a few of our men, two officers, and two guns, in company with a force under Brigadier Walpole, and marched for a river about ten miles off, near which the enemy are encamped and in great force.

January 14th, Friday.—This morning we struck tents, and the whole force moved to another camping ground, rather further away from the town, which is very pleasant after having been encamped on the same ground for so long.

January 15th, Friday.—To-day, Lieutenant Vaughan, with another party of our men, and two 24-pounders, left the camp to join the force under Brigadier Walpole, and where Lieutenant Hay has already gone. Captain Peel often rides over to the camp where they are, and takes Lascelles and myself with him. Captain Jones also often goes with us, and we have capital rides. Brigadier Walpole's encampment is on the bank of a river, and facing the enemy, who are encamped round, and in a village about 900 yards on the other side of the river. We have got our guns in position close to the water on the bank, and they keep up an occasional fire on the village, which the enemy return, but without much damage. We have as yet got no means of crossing the river, without which we could not attack the enemy.

January 16th, Saturday.—This afternoon we marched out, and exercised as skirmishers. We rode over to the river, where the rest of our men are, one afternoon, Captain Peel among the party, and as we were standing close to one of our guns we saw a native come running towards us from the village where the enemy were. Every one took it for granted that he was a spy, and let him come close up to the opposite bank of the river, when, after taking a good look round at us, and our guns, &c., he turned round and ran off towards the village as hard as he could pelt. Of course then everyone began to fire, but were so taken by surprise that not a bullet touched him, and getting a good way off, he turned round and waved his turban at us in derision. The Captain got a lot of casks together, and has had them lashed together, and made into a kind of floating bridge, by which there would be no difficulty in crossing the river, but there have been no orders to advance.

January 17th, Sunday.—This morning we marched over to the Royal Artillery parade ground, where our chaplain read the service.

January 18th, Monday.—This afternoon we buried one of our gunner's mates, named Oates, who died of dysentery and was one of our very best men. We buried him in a quiet place surrounded by a wall, close to the parade ground of the 93rd Highlanders, and where they were drilling at the time, but as soon as they saw our funeral they dismissed at once, and all their officers immediately came and joined us, and attended through all the service. Our men have always been greater chums with the 93rd Highlanders than with any other regiment, although they are on excellent terms with the whole of them.

January 19th, Tuesday.—This afternoon we marched out and had some exercise as skirmishers, &c. We occasionally ride into Surrackabad, which is a very curious and large town, close to Soorutghurh, the latter consisting of very little else besides the fort, which is being strengthened very much by the Royal Engineers, and all the thick wood and trees around it, among which an enemy might be concealed, in case of an attack are being cut down. A good many houses belonging to the natives are being cleared away also, that are near the walls of the fort, to the great dismay of the inhabitants; but they are always quartered in some other huts.

January 20th, Wednesday.—No news yet about the force encamped near the river, as to whether they are to cross over and advance on the enemy or not, but it is rumoured that they will not do so at all, and that the force is only stationed there to keep the enemy in check.

January 21st, Thursday.—We keep up a daily communication with the force by the river side, and one afternoon two of our midshipmen were riding over there from our camp, and had a dispute half way as to which was the right road, so they settled by separating, and each of them took his own road. The one that was right arrived in good time and remained until it was getting dark, but heard nothing of his companion when it was time to return to our camp, and had to go back without him. We all thought that some of the enemy must have got hold of him, and they were just going to order out some sowars to scour the country round when he made his appearance, having lost himself, and made an immense round. One of our engineers got fired at also, in riding across from behind a house in a village.

January 22nd, Friday.—Had a march out again in the afternoon. and some exercise. It is reported that we are to wait for a convoy of guns, stores, &c., which is on its way down from Agra, before we march for Cawnpore.

January 23rd, Saturday.—Our usual parades, &c., to-day.

The force at the river is still stationary, and only exchange from 20 to 30 shots with the enemy during the day, but without much damage on either side. None of our blue jackets have got wounded, and very few soldiers, and two or three bullocks killed. As soon as the enemy open fire our guns reply, but never commence, as without advancing, which they cannot do, they can do no good.

January 24th, Sunday.—This morning we marched over to the Artillery's parade ground, and had service with them, which was read by Mr. Bowman, they not having a chaplain with them.

January 25th, Monday.—Had a march this afternoon and drill. There are a good many sales of things that have been left in the town of Surrachabad going on, the enemy went in such a hurry that a good deal was left behind them. The Nawab of Surrachabad's palace is a beautiful place and splendidly situated. It is being undermined by the sappers, and is to be blown up. He left a beautiful tiger and tigress in a large cage in his garden. There are also splendid groves of orange trees there, and we had great fun one day there, when a good many of us, including the captain, had ridden over, and we began pelting each other with oranges on horseback, and the captain got his share as well as the others. After this we filled our pockets and amused ourselves by pelting all the parrier dogs we came across on our way home.

January 26th, Tuesday.—There are rumours to-day of the enemy collecting themselves together near Mhow, where Lieutenant Young, with a party of our men and a force went to before, but did not come across them.

January 27th, Wednesday.—Marched out this afternoon

and drilled. Late this evening the 53rd regiment, and a small force were ordered off with four day's provisions for Mhow, where the enemy are re-assembling, and we expect to hear of their having a brush.

January 28th, Thursday.—There are rumours that we shall march soon, as the convoy from the Assa is within a day or two's march.

January 29th, Friday.—The 53rd and force returned from Mhow this afternoon, having had a stout engagement with the enemy close to Mhow. The enemy were driven back with 400 killed and the loss of four guns; the loss on our side was trifling, but unfortunately a tumbril full of ammunition blew up, which killed several men. Hodson's horse made a charge, in which their officers, the men being all natives, were not properly supported, and consequently a good many of their officers got wounded.

January 30th, Saturday.—This afternoon we marched out for exercise and had some drill. Rumours are current to the effect that we shall march soon for Cawnpore, but nothing is known for certain.

January 31st, Sunday.—The 53rd regiment and a detachment of the 42nd Highlanders marched over to our camp this morning, and formed square with us for church. In the order book this evening there are orders for us to march to-morrow morning at five. We are all glad of it, as we have been encamped here so long, but it comes rather hard having to turn out so early in the morning, after having been encamped in comparative idleness for so long.

February 1st, Monday.—This morning at five o'clock the grunting of camels and knocking out of tent-pegs proclaimed that we were off again. By half-past six we were in our station on the road, and soon afterwards the advance sounded. After a march of about twelve miles, we encamped about a mile on the Soorutgurh side of the river Kalla Nudda, where our action after 2nd of January took place. We have now got the Queen's Bays with us, who are a great addition to the army, as we have so little European cavalry. They are under command of Brigadier Campbell, who joined our mess when we messed together at Allahabad.

February 2nd, Tuesday.—Struck tents at six o'clock this morning, and proceeded on our march. We crossed the bridge over the Kalla Nudda, the scene of our late skirmish, and through the village which we had bombarded. The walls and houses were regularly riddled in some places, and a good many skeletons laying about. About one p.m. we arrived and encamped at Gourjeanah. One of the most disagreeable parts of a march is the waiting for the baggage after our arrival at the new camping ground. We sometimes have to wait for two or three hours in the burning sun, and if it happens to be in a dusty field or plain, it makes it worse. A few marines are always told off to pitch our tent with the assistance of our native servants. We always keep a sharp look out on our elephant, the bearer of the tent, during the march, and see that he is not allowed to lag behind, so ours is generally up sooner than the others. It is generally a race between our tent and the captain's, as his steward always remains with his during the march, so it is always up in good time.

February 3rd, Wednesday.—Struck tents and marched

again at six this morning, and arrived after a ten miles march at Meereah Ka Saraie. There are a good many of the enemy hanging about the villages in small parties, and they are continually getting taken up. Mr. Bowman and Lascelles went out shooting, and in a village through which they passed, they were met by some Sheiks, who made some signs to them to follow them, and led them to a house where they found two regular Sepoys armed. They tried to make some resistance, but one fellow got a tremendous gash from one of the Sheik's turrawhars, and the other one was taken prisoner, and brought into camp.

February 4th, Thursday.—Struck tents and started again at five this morning, and arrived at eleven o'clock and encamped at a place called Rukown. As an instance of the scoundrels the natives are, a syre (native groom) of mine ran from me in a most provoking way. After striking tents in the morning, and when the men have fallen in and everything is ready for marching, the captain always mounts his horse, and Lascelles and myself as aides-de-camp do the same. At this time I went to the place where my pony had been piqueted for the night, expecting to find my syre waiting for me with the pony ready saddled, but to my astonishment I found the pony still fast to his peg, where he had been made fast for the night, and no sign of his being saddled or anything else, and the syre nowhere to be found; so I had to saddle him myself, and trust to any nigger I could get hold of to look after him on the march when I did not want him. I had aways treated the man well, and he ran away without the slightest provocation. Many of these native servants have run from their masters in the same way. You can never trust them for an instant; there have been cases in which native servants have got really attached to their masters, and can be trusted, but very seldom.

February 5th, Friday.—Struck tents at five o'clock this morning, and arrived about two o'clock at Poonah. There is not much to vary these marches, as we are going over the same ground that we did on our way to Cattagpore. Now and then we have an alarm, but they generally turn out to be only a few of the enemy's cavalry, who make themselves scarce as soon as they are observed. A detachment of our cavalry is generally sent to scour the country round where we intend to camp, before the tents are pitched.

February 6th, Saturday.—Struck tents as usual at five this morning, and encamped at Choubapore, which place is about 12 miles from Cawnpore. We have got numbers of camp followers attached, especially to the Naval Brigade, such as beastie wallahs, and cooks, &c. for the men. Among them is a native, who sells cakes always on the march. He goes up and down the whole line, calling out "March and march," "Paste and paste," "Palk and palk," "Very good plum cake sar," which is about all the English he knows. He is a particular favourite of the Blue Jackets, and is called "Funny Green" by them always.

February 7th, Sunday.—Struck tents at five again this morning, and arrived about half-past twelve on the parade ground at Cawnpore. Here we found R. and C., who had been left behind with one company of our men when we marched for Cawnpore. Lieutenant

Salmon, who was sent down to Allahabad wounded, has also joined again, and taken command of the company. They have been in the entrenched camp, the same place where we were with Lieutenant Hay, while the relief of Lucknow was going on, and where we came in for General Wyndham's action. The report is that we shall soon march all together for Lucknow, for the final capture of the city. The 8-inch guns, six in number, which the captain wrote for to Allahabad, have arrived, and the carriages which we brought down from Soorutgurh are all completed, and the guns are to be mounted at once, so that we shall be able to take them with us to Lucknow. They have often been in communication with General Outram's force, which has been in the Alumbagh at Lucknow, since Sir Colin Campbell left the town, after they had relieved the garrison. They have had almost daily actions with the enemy, who are in the town, and scarcely leave them alone, night or day. they, however, have resisted every attack as yet, but of course have suffered severely.

February 8th, Monday.—We have had a fatigue party at work the whole of the day in the entrenched camp. mounting the 8-inch guns. Mr. Bowman, Lascelles, and myself went up to see Mr. Moore, who we stayed with when we were here before. We found Dangerfield still with him, and not knowing exactly what to do with himself. Men are employed in all directions making fascines, &c., and getting everything ready for a move at once.

February 9th, Tuesday.—Regiments are daily moving off towards Lucknow, all having orders to encamp at different places on the way, so as to line the road, and be ready to close up and advance together on Lucknow when everything is ready.

February 10th, Wednesday.—We finished mounting our 8-inch guns to-day, and are now ready for marching. The rest of our men (whom we left by the river at Soorutgurh under command of our first lieutenant Vaughan, and with Brigadier Walpole's force), are expected down soon. The weather is commencing to get hotter again; throughout the "cold season" it has always been dreadfully hot during the day, but cool in the evenings, and sometimes even cold at night.

February 11th, Thursday.—The rifle brigade, 23rd regiment, and the remainder of our men, with 4-pounders arrived to-day from Soorutgurh under command of Brigadier Walpole, having left the river side according to orders, without either molesting or being molested by the enemy any more than they were before. The object of their having been detained seems to have been to protect our rear on our march down, and prevent them from advancing on us and crossing the river.

February 12th, Friday.—According to orders received last night, we struck tents at half-past four this morning, and marched off on the Lucknow road, in company with the 53rd regiment. We had some delay in getting the baggage, &c., and guns over the bridge, but once clear of that, we were able to go ahead a good pace, and arrived at a village called Ounow, near which we encamped, after a march of 12 miles. We found a small force of different regiments already encamped here. We are likely it is said to remain here for some while, until the whole force is clear of Cawnpore.

February 13th, Saturday.—Just after our parade this morning, the right wing of the 93rd Highlanders arrived and encamped next to us. They marched in in splendid style, and as they passed us our band was turned out and played a tune as a compliment to them. We are under strict orders never to leave the camp without arms of some description, and on no account to go outside the piquets, which are stationed about half-a-mile out on each side of our camp, so that our space to ride about in is rather limited. The reason of these orders is that the enemy are close round us on all sides, and they are hovering about in small bodies of cavalry, ready to pounce upon any stragglers. We have now got a most formidable battery (consisting of the siege train, which are eight 24-pounders, and six 8-inch guns, and two 8-inch howitzers, besides eight rocket tubes, making 16 guns, not counting the rockets.) The captain intends to establish a regular drill for the whole battery, which will be good practice and exercise for the men if we have to remain here long.

February 14th, Sunday.—The Royal Artillery with their guns are encamped close to us. Their guns are mostly 24-pounder siege train ones. We formed a square with the Royal Artillery and 53rd Regiments this morning and had church. We have got a good open space for a parade ground, close to our tents, and where we have packed our guns. Great care is always taken after the march in packing the guns, which is forming them in a good line, and sometimes in a square, with their tumbrils and ammunition waggons in the rear of each gun. If this is done well and orderly it looks neat, and tends to the credit of the corps to whom they belong.

February 15th, Monday.—Our usual parade to-day, and nothing particular occurred. After evening parade, we generally sally out, about 20 of us together, and have a regular good scamper on our ponies, lieutenants and all, which is great fun. Ounow is a small, but curious old village, with a good many curious kind of temples round it. In one of them we found an old bell, which we took, as we consider we have a right to appropriate to ourselves anything that we can pick up about here. Our encampment is within a few hundred yards of where one of General Havelock's actions took place, when he was on the way to Lucknow to relieve the garrison for the first time.

February 16th, Tuesday.—We are continually having alarms here, as the country round us is so crowded with the enemy. One morning, just after we had dismissed from parade, two or three videts, who had been stationed about a mile outside the camp, came galloping in with news that the enemy was advancing on us. The alarm was at once sounded, and the regiments all turned out, our men getting our guns ready for action. The 9th Lancers, who are with us now, were ordered out, and galloped off across the plain, and were soon out of sight, and among the clouds of dust, while we were all anxiously listening for the sound of a gun, and some fancied they could see some of the enemy's cavalry; however the Lancers returned with some horse artillery, which had also been sent out, after being away about an hour, but not having seen the enemy. They, however, met numbers of our camp followers, such as camel drivers, &c., running back into camp, having left their camels behind them in the hands of the enemy, so that they advanced very close to us. We often see some of their cavalry galloping about but in small parties.

February 17th, Wednesday.—This afternoon we had some battery drill, which consists of the whole battery of our guns being worked together, and exercised advancing, retreating, forming squares, &c., and pointing at different objects for practice. The guns are advanced, retreated, &c., by means of drag-ropes, which are manned by the gun-numbers. Eight-inch guns have never been seen worked in such a way on shore before, and the soldiers are quite astonished at it. Numbers of their officers also come and look on.

February 18th, Thursday.—Had some more battery drill this evening, which is to be our regular routine for the present, after evening parade. We got up some races one afternoon, by way of amusement for both officers and men. We had a long level piece of ground picked out for a race course, with fences and ditches made at intevals across it. We had great fun, and several races, both horse and foot. The former were by the officers on their ponies, and very good fun. The captain was umpire, and stationed at the winning post to proclaim the winners. Numbers of the army, both officers and men, were present, and different amusements went on among them. One was a pig with a greased tail, which had to be caught, and created great amusement. Our blue jackets also got hold of some bullocks which were near, and began racing with them, which was a most ridiculous thing, and created roars of laughter. Four or five men being on one unfortunate bullock, with three or four more hauling away at his tail, and perhaps some more at his horns. Captain Peel showed off his Arab Selim by leaping all the fences on the racecourse in splendid style.

February 19th, Friday.—Sir Hope Grant has been out with the 9th Lancers and 53rd regiment, and had an action near a place called Narwabjunge, in which they defeated the enemy, and captured their position with some guns. We heard the firing from our camp quite plainly, as they were not more than ten miles off.

February 20th, Saturday.—Sir Colin Campbell is expected soon to leave Cawnpore *en route* for Lucknow, and it is reported that all the attacking force will be reviewed at some place before advancing on the town.

February 21st, Sunday.—The 3rd battalion of the Rifle Brigade marched into camp this morning at 7 o'clock, with their band playing, and pitched their tents near us. We formed square with 93rd and 42nd Highlanders and Royal Artillery for church at eight this morning. Rumours are flying about that we shall move in a day or two.

February 22nd, Monday.—Our men are improving very much at their drill with the guns, and rattle them about famously. After the exercise for the evening is over, the drag-ropes are all manned, and the guns are run back into their places, with a lively tune playing from our band. The guns are then packed properly for the night.

February 23rd, Tuesday.—Lieutenant Wilson (with a few of our men, and a mid), has been encamped for some time at a place called Burmar. There are some of the 79th Highlanders with them. We expect they will join us after our next march, which will bring us near to where they are.

February 24th, Wednesday.—Orders came out in the order book this evening to march at five a.m. to-morrow. After our drill we got our guns in line facing the road, so as to be ready to move off quicker.

February 25th, Thursday.—Marched at five o'clock this morning, and encamped at ten o'clock at Narwabjunge. Orders came in the evening to march at daylight again to-morrow morning, which will take us within about 12 miles of Lucknow.

February 26th, Friday.—Marched again at half-past four this morning, and arrived and encamped on a large plain, four miles from Alumbagh, where the force under General Outram has been holding out ever since Sir Colin Campbell left Lucknow.

February 27th, Saturday.—Lieutenant Young and some of our Marine officers rode into the Allumbagh to-day, they found all the garrison getting on pretty well, but rather worn out with incessant fighting, as the enemy harass them day and night, and they are always under fire. As our party were coming into the Allumbagh under an arch, Lieutenant G——— said to our marine officer, who was in uniform, "Just see if your red jacket won't bring a shot down on us." He had scarcely spoken the words when a 24-pounder was fired at them, and the shot came rattling along just over their heads.

February 28th, Sunday.—Had church this morning at seven o'clock. Lieutenant Wilson and party has joined us now from Bermar. The weather is getting very hot and the regular hot season is begining to set in.

March 1st, Monday.—This afternoon Sir Colin Campbell rode over with his staff, and was present at our battery drill, at which he was extremely pleased, and expresssed his admiration at the way our men knocked their guns about.

March 2nd, Tuesday.—Captain Peel, Lieutenant Young, Salmon and Kerr, marched with four of our guns, and in company with some other regiments, at four o'clock this morning. The Captain said that as we should follow soon it was not worth while Lascelles and myself moving there, as it would break up our tent as all were not to go. We were just "turning in," and I was just getting into bed, when one of Sir Colin Campbell's aides-de-camp galloped up to Lieutenant Vaughan's tent (who was commanding officer in the captain's absence), and gave orders for us to march immediately. This was about half-past ten p.m., and rather unpleasant just as we thought we were going to have a good night's rest, but the excitement of the thought of being at Lucknow in a few hours time soon took all sleepiness away, and we were soon on the move. The nights are still rather chilly, although the days are much warmer. We were in full march by 11 o'clock, and marched the whole night. We went about five miles out of the way by missing a turn of the road, so that we did not arrive until ten o'clock the next morning, and encamped about a mile from the Dil-koosha.

March 3rd, Wednesday.—We were all dead beat after we arrived after our march, which lasted 12 hours, and very wearisome work being dark all the while. I found myself often dropping off to sleep while riding, and very nearly fell off a good many times. We pitched tents about a mile from the Dil-koosha or "heart's delight," a large palace which we found already occupied by our troops, they having already captured it from the enemy, so that luckily our tents were pitched out of the enemy's range. After a snooze and something to eat, Lascelles and I went up to where our four guns that preceded us were stationed, about two or three hundred yards the other side of the Dil-koosha, and commanding the Martinere, a large building which was strongly entrenched and fortified and crowded with the enemy. Our guns were keeping up a heavy fire on it, which was being returned smartly by the enemy. Two of our bluejackets were mortally wounded to-day; one of them was a boatswain's mate, and one of the best men in the ship; it is impossible that either of them can live. We found Captain Peel by the guns, and we were employed attending on him the rest of the afternoon, during which time we were under a very heavy fire from the enemy's guns, but we returned the compliment, and they got as good as they gave us. Occasionally they sent out clouds of skirmishers, which began firing away on us, but did very little harm, except two or three wounded among the soldiers. We returned to our camp in the evening, a party under Lieutenant Young were left in charge of the guns. From the place where they were stationed, we got a splendid view over the town, which was a beautiful sight, as it contains so many large buildings and domes, &c.

March 4th, Thursday.—Our guns and party were withdrawn from opposite the Martinere this morning, some of the Royal Artillery taking their places. The encampment of the whole of our force takes up an enormous space of ground now, and stretches close up to the Dil-koosha, so consequently some of the foremost tents are under fire, as the enemy's shot from the Martinere reaches them, that place being only about 900 yards from the Dil-koosha. After parade we rode up with the captain to the Dil-koosha, while the former got into a yarn with an artillery officer, and they both went out two or three hundred yards to the front and stood behind a tree examining some of the enemy who were firing muskets from a trench. The latter observed them, and directed their fire on them, but luckily without hitting either. The enemy kept on firing round shot at our artillery-men. and they came rattling down about our ears, but they were being sharply replied to.

March 5th, Friday.—This morning two of our 24-pounders, under command of Lieutenant Wilson, were sent to take up a position on the banks of the river Goomptee, to the right of the town, but within fire of the Martinere, and facing the enemy's position, whose camp stretch away for about half-a-mile on the right of the town. The captain, Lascelles, and myself accompanied Lieutenant Wilson and our men, and went down to the river with them. Just as we got clear of some trees, (while we were marching down to take up our position,) the enemy got a sight of us, and one of their guns let fly at us from the Martinere, as we could not return it till were in our place, and as the shot went down over us we hurried on, and after passing across a large field we arrived at the bank of the river, and our two guns were got into position close to a bridge which goes across the river. The guns from the Martinere opened on us at once, but as they had to encounter the fire from ours at the Dil-koosha they did not trouble us much, until some guns opened on us in front, which they had had concealed behind some trees. Several cavalry also made their appearance, who seemed to be covering their guns. The enemy had also posession of a village which they had strengthened very much, and from there they kept up a fire on us, but making very bad shots, but the guns they had posted behind the trees on our front annoyed us very much. Our guns were run close up to the edge of the bank, and some of their shot stuck in the slope of the bank, just under the muzzles of our guns. The 53rd regiment supported our guns, and kept up a fire of musketry wherever there was a chance. Later in the day the Royal Artillery got two of their guns in position to the left of ours. One particular gun at one corner of the Martinere annoyed us most; they worked it very cleverly, and had a capital place for it, so that the gun was only visible just at the moment of firing, and the instant it was fired it was run in, and sponged and loaded behind the corner of the wall, and out of our sight. Both our guns and the Royal Artillery's kept up an incessant fire on it the whole day, and knocked away a great deal of the wall, but could not silence the gun.

March 6th, Saturday.—Early this morning General Outram with a large force crossed over the Goomptee, by the bridge which our guns are protecting for the purpose of attacking the town on its right flank. They met the enemy close to the village opposite our guns, and had a severe engagement and drove the enemy before them for some way. The Queen's Bays composed part of the force, and they made a brilliant charge, but not without the loss of a good many men, and one of their majors, who was shot dead. It was the first time they had had a good opportunity of distinguishing themselves, and their charge was rather a rash one. After the engagement General Outram posted his guns, and immediately began cannonading the town, so that they were attacked both in front and on their right. The 53rd regiment have stationed a piquet a little way on the opposite side of the river, and close to the bridge. They keep up an incessant fire of musketry from there, as the enemy, taking advantage of some long grass in a large field in front of them, try and creep up close. The guns from the Martinere have been keeping up a heavy fire on us all day, and we are not able to do them much harm in return, as they are under such good cover. They have got small trenches and holes dug in the ground all round the Martinere, and they keep on firing away out of these trenches; all you see of them being puffs of smoke, and now and then a head or two. Occasionally they throw out masses of skirmishers, with no end of bugling, &c., but otherwise they keep well under cover. Their favourite time is when our piquets are being relieved, and then the piquets marching down to relieve and the one returning get a tremendous peppering. We are waiting now for Jung Bahadoor and his Ghoorkas, who are to attack the town on the other side; after their arrival the town will be surrounded.

March 7th, Sunday.—The cannonade commenced again this morning, and has been kept up on both sides the whole day. Our two blue-jackets that were mortally wounded have both died, and the captain has had a wooden cross put up over their graves. The Dil-koosha has been turned into a hospital for the wounded. It is a handy place for it, but until we take the Martinere, it will be under the enemy's fire.

March 8th, Monday.—To-day according to orders our guns were withdrawn from the river side. Jung Bahadoor and his men have arrived, and the former has had an interview with Sir Colin Campbell. The Ghoorkas are stout, short men, and look good for plenty of work with their muskets and knives; the latter are their chief weapons, and they are very clever at using them. We expect that we shall commence a regular attack to-morrow and advance into the town. The whole of our guns are ordered to be got ready.

March 9th, Tuesday.—At four o'clock this morning, we marched out of camp with four of our 8-inch guns and some rocket tubes, and took up our position in front of the Dil-koosha, and opposite to the Martinere, a little to the left of where our guns were before. It was quite dark when we arrived at our position, and the enemy appeared not to have observed us, so we set to work at once making an embankment with sand bags, &c., for a protection to the guns. Just in the rear of our battery some natives were set to work to dig a large trench, in which we put our ammunition. Our rocket tubes were drawn up in a line to the right of the guns. As it grew lighter the enemy soon observed us, and opened musketry from innumerable trenches all round the Martinere. A short while afterwards, some guns opened upon us, and the round shot began whistling over our heads, the corner gun, which we had tried so often to silence as lively as ever. We had to bear this for some little while without returning it, as our battery was not quite finished, and

Captain Peel said that he would not fire a single shot, until he got orders from Sir Colin to that effect. However the orders were soon brought to us by an aide-de-camp, and we commenced the cannonade at once. The enemy were in such crowds in their trenches, and so well concealed, that it was very hard to do them much damage. Several capital shots were made, and we burst a good many shell right in the middle of some of their trenches, lined with men. Their skirmishers could not do much, as they got driven back by our fire at once, but they kept up an incessant fire both of musketry and round shot the whole morning. About one o'clock I spied our native servant, who attended on us in our tent, coming down with some dinner, which was very acceptable, although I had to eat it sitting on the ground under a rocket cart; and a whistle of a shot flying over head every now and then made the mouthsful digest all the quicker. About two o'clock, the enemy still keeping up their fire, although we had been cannonading them the whole morning, we began firing Moorsoon shell on some buildings composed of small huts, &c., which were just outside of the Martinere, and crowded with the enemy. They did not seem to approve of the Moorsoon shell at all, which burst as soon as they struck their objects, and these outhouses were soon almost entirely deserted, except by about 80 Sepoys, who would not go at any price. We fired shell after shell right among them, but they still held their ground, and certainly behaved most pluckily. No one liked to call them plucky, but acknowledged they were very obstinate. About half-past two, Captain Peel went off some way to the left of the guns, and chose a position where we might get some of them in position, so as to attack the place from the left. This accordingly was done, and the enemy began to get very discomforted at the fire they were under, both from our guns on their front, and on their right. After this had been going on for some while, Captain Peel sent me a message back from the camp about some reinforcements, and in the meantime went some way on foot in front of our two guns on the left to reconnoitre the enemy's position. All this while they were keeping up a heavy fire from their trenches, and taking advantage of the ground by creeping up behind hillocks, &c., and getting as close to our guns as possible. While Captain Peel was standing up looking at the enemy, but not noticing some of the nearest who were firing at him for some time, one of them at length made a good shot, but a very bad one for us, and hit him in the thigh with a musket ball. Just after he was hit, I came in sight of our guns and dismounted, having ridden from the camp, and began walking down towards our men, when I saw a crowd of blue-jackets and some of our officers together in one place, so I guessed at once that someone was wounded, and went back to the Dil-koosha and got a dhoolie and ran with it down to our men, where I found out who it was. He was lifted into the dhoolie, and taken at once to the Dil-koosha. It was very hot, and the wound made him weak and faint at once, so they put on a blue-jacket's broad brimmed white hat to keep the sun off him better, and took his coat off; it was in this state I found him when I got down with the dhoolie, and I could scarcely believe that it was he at first, he looked so changed, and his face as white as a sheet. Dr. Grant, the

surgeon of the 93rd Higlanders, extracted the ball, which
had stuck in his right thigh. He was put into a room in
the Dil-koosha by himself, and Lascelles and myself went
up by turns and stayed with him; he was in great pain
for some while after the operation. His being wounded
has cast a gloom over all of us, both officers and men, as
he so entirely kept the whole thing going, however we
are in hopes of his being all right again in about three
weeks time. Lieutenant Vaughan, first lieutenant, is in
command of the brigade now, until the captain is fit for
duty. We kept up the cannonade until four o'clock, when
orders came from Sir Colin Campbell for the storming
party to hold themselves in readiness. Our fire in the
meanwhile increased, and soon afterwards the storming
party (the most prominent regiment of it being the 93rd
Highlanders) received orders to advance. As soon as
they moved forward, we recommenced our fire with if
possible, renewed vigour, and kept on firing as fast as
possible so as to confuse the enemy. The storming party
steadily advanced, and when they got pretty close, broke
off into skirmishing order and moved on faster. It was
one of the prettiest sights I have ever seen, their advancing
in twos and threes in a bunch, and every now and then a
shell bursting or a shot knocking up the dust between
them. When they got close up to the enemy, we ceased
firing for fear of our shot getting among our own men.
They then made a rush forward, and the enemy, after a
few irregular volleys from their trenches, got up from
them and ran, deserting all their trenches, the huts in
front, and the whole of the Martinere with guns. The
Highlanders instantly took possession, and we hailed the

event with loud cheering. One great thing in the capture of the Martinere is that the Dil-koosha, where there are so many wounded, will for the future be out of fire, which will be a great comfort for the sick. After the Highlanders took possession, they met the enemy on the other side, and had some smart skirmishing, in which they had several killed and wounded. Our guns were advanced at once, and got in position on the other side of the Martinere, though there was a great deal of difficulty in getting them there in consequence of the numerous trenches and holes dug by the enemy. I examined some of them, they were capitally dug out, some of them regular burrows with just room for a couple of men, and a space left for their muskets. In the evening Captain Peel was taken back to the camp in a dhoolie, and put into his own tent. I went back with him, and that evening felt the first commencement of fever. I had been riding and running about the whole day, going messages backwards and forwards from where we were engaged to our camp, and all this in the hottest part of the day, so that when I got back to camp, I felt fairly knocked up, and dreamed all manner of disagreeable dreams after I turned in.

March 10th, Wednesday.—This morning I woke up feeling very unwell, but determined not to give in to it if I could possibly help it. About nine o'clock, orders came down for us to remove our camp to the rear of the Dil-koosha. The captain was moved back again to the Dil-koosha and put into the room he was in before, and where he will be kept alone. I managed to get over to our new encampment all right, but after the captain had been lodged in his room, and our tent pitched, I felt so ill that I fairly gave way to it and had to lay down on my bed. The fire was kept up the whole day, and an important position, consisting of a house called Bank's Bungalow, was taken from the enemy, and our guns advanced beyond it.

March 11th, Thursday.—After to-day I felt so ill that I had to give up keeping a daily journal, and in fact, everything else, as I was too weak and miserable to do anything. To-day the Bejum Kotee was captured after a bombardment from our guns, the storming party being composed of the 93rd Highlanders and the Sattanpore regiment.

On the 12th the Emanbana was attacked, and two of our guns were got into position close to the walls of it, and on the 14th it was captured, and also the Keiserbagh. In the latter place an immense quantity of loot was found, and an enormous number of jewels and articles of great value were found. On the 15th the Mess House was captured, and on the 16th the great Emanbana. On the 17th the last body of rebels left the city, and it was a case of pursuing columns of cavalry. Brigadier Campbell, the commandant of the Queen's Bays, got into trouble at this time, as he was ordered to go to a certain part of the town to cut off an immense body of the rebels who were flocking out, and not being able to find out the right place, he got a guide to show him, who took him quite in a different direction, being a native spy, and consequently the whole of this body of the enemy escaped. During the latter part, while the fighting was going on in the town, I was scarcely able to move about in my tent, but used just to sit outside a little in the evening and watch the shells bursting over the town. During the latter part there were a good many explosions from mines, which the enemy had laid; a great many of the Ghoorkas were blown up by them. The latter have not behaved very well on the whole as to bravery; on one occasion the only way that they could make them advance was by the Highlanders threatening to shoot them if they didn't. After the town was considered evacuated, a good many parties of both officers and men used to go about the town in search of loot, &c., and the misfortunes they met with proved that a good many of the enemy were lurking about, long after it was thought to be cleared. Several, both officers and men, were killed in this way, and a number of them had very narrow escapes. We discharged a sergeant of the 78th Highlanders, who had been attached to us, to assist in drilling the men, and as he was on the way to join his regiment, and going through the town after leaving us, he was attacked by half a dozen Sepoys, and was obliged to run for his life, leaving a camel with everything he had in the hands of the enemy, so we got up a subscription for him. Captain Peel has been during this time in the room in the Dil-koosha, and his wound progresses slowly but well, but the doctors say that it will be some time before he will be able to get about. The last few days before we left Lucknow, he was able to be taken about in a dhoolie a little, and he was afterwards taken into the hospital, where he could be better looked after than in the Dil-koosha. I got rid of the actual fever before we marched, which we did at the end of the month, but I was still so very weak from it, that I was obliged to be carried in a dhoolie during the march. This is a most disagreeable process, as you are left entirely to the mercy of the four dhoolie bearers who carry you, and as you cannot see either behind or before you, and only a little on either side, if you keep the blind drawn, it is rather nervous work, especially in a crowd on the march, and where you have elephants, camels, mules, and horses all round you. We left the captain behind, who was in great hopes of following us soon, as we got orders to march down and embark as soon as we could. We travelled from Cawnpore to Allahabad by the bullock waggons, which is a most uncomfortable way of travelling. We remained at Cawnpore for a few days before going on to Allahabad, and I had great hopes at the former place of being well enough to go back to my duty again, but just after I got much better, I fell ill again with a bad cough, and got more weak than ever. We had a miserable journey from Cawnpore to Allahabad by these bullock waggons, and as we had no tents with us, we had of course to sleep, &c., in the waggons, which hold just two people with their charpoys (bedsteads) and some baggage. We halted occasionally in the day, and then we had to get under trees or any shady place we could find to cook our food, and wash, &c. I was scarcely able to move, and just managed to creep under a tree and lie down till it was ready to go on again. We came down with only part of our men under Lieutenant Hay, the rest being behind and the assistant surgeon with them; so we had only an apothecary, a half-cast, who looked after me however very well, and gave me lots of port wine, &c., to keep me up, and certainly I think doctored me quite as well as the surgeon would have done. The hot winds of the season also began to blow; they were perfectly scorching, and accompanied by tremendous clouds of blinding dust. We got in this way to within about 60 miles of Allahabad, to which place we went by rail. The railway carriage was so dreadfully hot, and altogether I felt so ill that when we arrived I felt more dead than alive. We found Lieutenant Vaughan and some of our men there, who had gone on before us. I was put at once into a dhoolie, and taken to a tent which we found already pitched for us. Dr. Beale, who came up with us at first, and who was left in charge of our depot of sick, we also found here. When I got to the tent the thermometer was at 105, under the canvas. Dr. Beale was very kind to me, and took me to his house which he had been living in all the while. Mr. Bowman also went there, and another mid who was ill. I remained there a day until Dr. Beale made arrangements for my going down to Calcutta at once with the other mid by dôk, as he said it was very necessary for me to get proper care at once. We set off in the evening by dôk, a small carriage with just room for us two to lie down at full length, but scarcely for us to turn round. We took about five days going down to Raneegunge in this way. There are small inns and resting houses all along the road at the end of each stage, on purpose for travellers by the dôk, and we stopped at these during the great heat of the day, and got something to eat and rested, and then started again in the evening, and travelled all night, sleeping as well as we could in our carriage. This was most wretched work, but the nearer we got to Calcutta, the less grew the hot winds, which was a great relief. We got hold of a Captain Maxwell, who was brother to a

Major Maxwell, who was interpreter to us for some while, and when he found out who we were, he was very kind to us, and sent me some soda-water and different things, when we met at the resting houses as we were travelling down to Calcutta, the same way, and with him his wife. We went to an hotel at Raneegunge when we got there, and then by the railway to Calcutta. I began to feel a little better, and actually made a kind of breakfast at the hotel at Raneegunge. It was such a great relief getting away from the hot winds, which very seldon blow badly so far south. On arrival at Calcutta, we got a boat and went on board the "Shannon," where we found the master who had been left in charge of the ship, with three or four officers. They seemed quite worn out and bored with the length of time they had been at Calcutta, and all of them seemed more or less ill. Another of our surgeons whom we left behind was also on board, and he went on shore at once to the officers' sick quarters in Little Repull Street, and settled about our being taken in there. It seemed very odd being on board ship again and I could scarcely believe it when I thought of all I had seen and gone through since I was on board last. In the evening after the heat of the day, the assistant surgeon got a gany for us, and we went to the sick quarters, which we found to be a most comfortable house, and with very few officers in just then. We first come to a large room which had been turned into a kind of ward, and lots of beds put into it, and the matron was going to show us upstairs for us to see if we should like the rooms up there, and to choose one to ourselves, but I felt so ill and tired that I lay down on the first bed I came across and said I would not move for anybody, so consequently I was located in a big room and the mid who was with me also. I was very comfortable indeed there, and made great friends at once with a Captain Stewart, who was wounded, and in the next bed to me. Our intimacy began by my apologising to him for my cough, as I was afraid it might keep him awake, and from that we got into conversation. Lintwood, the doctor, lived in the house, and was a very good one, and very kind to me. A few days afterwards I heard of poor Captain Peel being taken ill, and shortly afterwards the doctor told me of his death. I never felt, till I actually heard of the event, what a really kind friend he had been to me; he had always been especially kind to me, and was liked by all, and the loss indeed was a dreadful one. He had intended before his death to have written a general summary to the Lords of the Admiralty of the proceedings of the Naval Brigade, and mentioning the individual acts of each officer belonging to it, which unfortunately he was unable to do before his death. Lieutenant Vaughan after wrote to the Admiralty mentioning those officers who had not been especially mentioned before by the captain, and so I hope to be able to make it a claim for promotion, as the whole of our lieutenants were promoted to commanders, and all those who could be promoted were. I also heard that the Naval Brigade had been detained at Ghza, a place about 40 miles from Raneegunge. The reason for their being detained was that a large force of Sepoys under one of their great chiefs, Koee-Ling, was hovering about. Our men remained there for three months without coming in contact with the enemy at all, except a slight skirmish of a small party of our men under Captain Young, one of our promoted lieutenants. Our men laid in ambush, and cut up the whole of the enemy, about 50 in number, with their cutlasses. Otherwise they had nothing whatever to do, and all this while I was in the sick quarters and getting on very comfortably. I got one relapse and a very bad attack of fever again, but the doctor was very kind and attended on me very well. I used sometimes when I got stronger to get up at five o'clock in the morning and watch the volunteers at drill, and then in the evening I used to have a drive. In the beginning of August our men came down, and about 50 of those who had been sent down from up country, sick and wounded, who were well enough, were formed into a kind of company, and two other officers besides myself, who had been sent down sick, took command of them, and joined the rest at the station on their arrival. We then marched through the town to the ship, and were received by the inhabitants in a most splendid manner, salutes firing in all directions, and all the house-tops lined with people. The whole of the regiments in the town and the crew of the "Pylades," another man-of-war frigate, were drawn up on either side of the road, and presented arms as we passed, the bands playing "Rule Britannia." As soon as the men got on board, they manned the rigging according to orders, and gave three cheers. Sir James Outram came on board, and we were all presented to him on the quarter deck. Unfortunately 130 men under Captain Young did not arrive till a few days after, so that they did not come in for the grand reception. A short time afterwards the inhabitants gave a grand dinner to our men in the town hall, which passed off very well. We sailed on the 17th September, under Commander Marten, who had been given the temporary rank of captain to take the ship home. It was a general source of great regret that poor Sir William Peel should not have lived to take his ship home, which was a most earnest wish of both him and all his officers and men, We left Calcutta heartily glad at the prospect of getting away from the heat and mosquitoes, but not without feelings of regret at leaving the country where we had gone through so much danger and excitement, and where, as at Calcutta, a great deal of kindness had been shown us.

LETTERS FROM INDIA.

RIVER GANGES,
September 17th, 1857.

DEAR——
We are not likely to arrive at Allahabad for the next week, but I may as well begin my letter now, and by the time we arrive I daresay I shall have remembered all the things I want to tell you. The first lieutenant and Vaughan have left Calcutta with 100 more men and six officers of the "Shannon," and I shouldn't be surprised if he were to bring letters up with him, but the mail may not have come in. The "Mirzapoor" and the steamer we are in arrived at Dinapore, last Friday, the 4th. We had a very busy day of it, embarking and getting all the baggage on board. I had a great deal to do attending on the captain, running about in the sun and so on, that when I came back to barracks, as we were not to go on board till next morning, I was quite knocked up and very feverish. The doctor saw me and said he would give me some medicine. The next morning I was better, but I got

unwell again the next day, and I had to go through pills and castor oil and all that sort of thing, but am now quite well again. I was about the only one who had not been ill before coming up, so that it was fairly my turn, but I soon got over it. Clinton is regularly laid up, but I hope he will soon be all right again. Mr. Bowman nursed me when I was ill, and as soon as I got well he fell ill, and is very unwell now, but I assure you I make a beautiful nurse. I did not tell you in my letter from Dinapore that I wrote a letter from Calcutta before we left, saying that I was going in the Naval Brigade, and gave it to the clerk to send home; I hope you have got it all right. I have so many things to tell you that I am afraid I shall not remember half, but I will try; I don't think I gave you a description of our arriving at Calcutta in either of my last two letters.

We arrived on a very hot afternoon on the 2nd of August, two or three days after I wrote to you. "Steaming up the River Hoogly" we had most beautiful scenery the whole way. Such curious ships of all nations, and American steamers with engines on the upper deck, and boats full of natives fishing and yelling at us like fun, it was really very interesting. All the signal stations on shore kept signalling to us "what ship?" and "what troops?" and so Lord Elgin put another two or three hundred on to the number of men, so as to keep their spirits up every time we answered them. Well, it was about four o'clock when we arrived at Calcutta, the shore perfectly crowded. There were hundreds and hundreds of merchant ships there, some beautiful vessels: French, Dutch, Yankee, and all kinds. We passed the "Himalaya,"

looking as big as ever, and anchored opposite an immense
ghaut or landing-place, and fired our salute. Then you
should have seen the fun, horses running away, carriages
coming down by the run, such a hubbub; they evidently did
not expect it at all. I had no idea Calcutta was such a large
place. It is quite immense, with some beautiful buildings
in it, among which is the Governor-General's palace, a
magnificent one. Swells of different kinds kept pouring
on board the whole evening, quite thunder-struck with
the size of the ship. No ship with as much tonnage (2662
tons) as we are, has ever got up as far as Calcutta before.
I told you in my letter from Calcutta how I went to the
Governor of Bengal's house, but Captain James was gone
away. I have got his direction, but have not yet been
able to write to him. I think I also told you that the
Bishop and Governor-General came on board to inspect
the Naval Brigade. Just before we disembarked, Lord
Elgin came on board, and made the jolliest speech I ever
heard. We embarked on board the steamer all right. I
said good-bye to everyone, including the first lieutenant,
who shook hands, and said laughing "Well, who have
you left all your things to; you don't expect ever to come
back, do you?" and thought he had made a very clever
joke, only it was getting rather old, because it was just
what everyone was saying to everyone else before. The
usual question was "Who's all your gear going to be left
to? I'll take care of it"; that's to say if he was getting
short of white trousers, he wouldn't scruple to take a pair
or two out of your chest; but I left mine to nobody, but
locked it up, and there it will have to stay till I come
back. There was very poor accommodation on board the

"Chunar" (the name of the steamer), but we soon managed to settle down and make ourselves comfortable. On first trying to go ahead the same evening that we embarked, we found that we were not able to do so, the engines being out of order, so we had to anchor for the night. We might just as well have been on board the "Shannon." The next morning we started again on board—heavy rain—but it did not prevent those left behind on board giving us three good cheers, as we passed them, which we answered heartily. We steamed on till about four o'clock that day, when we broke down again and had to anchor. Two days after that we anchored at at Barrackpore, the place where the mutiny among the Sepoys first began. They fired on their officers, and then made off with all the ammunition and everything else. The worst of these Sepoys is that they are used to the climate, and it does not affect them; besides they have run off with all their arms and ammunition, and have got plenty of artillery which we have not. There will be some hard fighting. I wish they would send troops out from England quicker, there are such thousands and thousands of these beggars about everywhere. At this place (Barrackpore), the captain telegraphed down to Calcutta to tell them to send up one of those American steamers called the "River Bird," which we had observed at anchor there. She came up the next morning, and we went steaming away in her. We were here much more comfortable than in the "Chunar," and she was a much better steamer. The scenery all about here was not very particular, and the land rather low and marshy, but every now and then we came upon some large bungalow, or

English private house, or sometimes a Hindoo temple, some of which are very handsome. We had to anchor every night, because it is not safe for any steamer to be on the river after dark. I will write down a list of all the places we anchored at, which I will get from my journal, so that you will be able to trace them in the map. Berhampore was one of the chief places. We stayed here two days, as the pilot said he could not possibly take us up. The captain was perfectly frantic, and there was no other steamer expected down for a week, so he determined we should go. He bothered and bothered till he drove the pilot almost crazy, but on the captain saying he would take the whole responsibility on himself, he gave in, and said he would take us up further, but we were sure to be smashed to pieces. This steamer was not made for the river, and drew a great deal more water than the others, so that was the reason why he wouldn't take us up further, and he had good reason to be afraid, as no steamer drawing so much water had ever been up further than this place before.

GHAZEEPORE,

September 27th.

HERE we are! in a very comfortable private gentleman's house, at a place called Ghazeepore, or as it is sometimes spelt Ghaziepore, celebrated for rose water. I will now tell you how we got here. A few days after we started from Dinapore, in the steamer "Mirzapore," we ran aground on a sandbank close to the shore. We tried everything that could be thought of to get her off, but could not succeed. There was another steamer in company with us to help us tow the flat, so the captain went on board of her with part of the men and two officers, took the flat in tow, and steamed up to this place, leaving us behind in the "Mirzapore" hard and fast on the sandbank. They were away three days from us. During that time the water gradually went away from us and the river was falling, till we were left high and dry on the shore.

The fellows had capital fun shooting on shore at jackals and dogs, but I was obliged to stay on board, as I was on the list with a bad foot. The doctor has not taken me out yet, but my foot is almost well; it was a kind of fester. Our port paddle-box was right out of water, resting on the bank, and we heeled over so tremendously on the other side, it looked quite curious outside to think how we could have lived on board of her. The jackals used to come howling under the paddle-box, and with the mosquitoes and cockroaches it was a very hard job to get to sleep at all at nights, so I was very glad when I saw the other steamer coming down to take the rest of us up. The captain came down in her and told us all the men were comfortably landed here in barracks, and that the officers were quartered at the house of a private gentleman who had gone to Allahabad, and in a short time the steamer will come for us. We expect it in about ten days time. We are very comfortable here, the only thing is we have no knives or forks or anything of that kind, so we have to scrape up anything we can get, which is great fun. I got hold of a large carving fork and a small tea spoon, with which I had to tear a mutton chop to pieces. The food they give us is very good, so it makes it all the more tantalizing, but I will buy a knife and fork here. We are put to a great deal of expense here on shore. I hope the government or the East India Company will make it good to us. We have to pay between six or eight shillings a day for the commonest keep possible. There are six of us. It is very lucky that I got five pounds battle money in advance before I left the "Shannon," for I don't know what I should have done without it. The East India Company or the government pay for our messing coming up in the steamer, so they ought to do so when we are on shore. I have got a very good bearer, or servant, here. He does every single thing for me, only he knows very little English. I want him to come to Allahabad with me, but I don't know whether I shall get him or not. If he does not, I shall have no servant of any kind whatever, and it would be very difficult, especially after a long march, to look after all my things. Most of the officers are going to take black servants up.

GHAZEEPORE,

October 2nd, 1857.

EVERTHING all right and very comfortable: hope you are the same. I must now go on with my description of my journey up here. I left off when I had arrived at Berhampore, and the captain had persuaded the pilot to take us up farther. We stayed here two days, and on the 27th August started again. On Friday, 28th August, we ran aground, but got off without damage. On Saturday, 29th August, early in the morning, a man fell overboard when it was blowing, and we were running hard before daylight. The boat was sent after him, and went off a tremendous rate with the current, but we soon lost sight of her in the dark. We heard the man shouting two or three times, but could not hear what he said. We had given up all hopes of the man's life, as we did not expect the boat could find him in the dark. We waited a whole hour, when it got lighter, and we spied the boat pulling back; they had the man safe. It was a most wonderful escape: he was in the water about a quarter of an hour, and the current washed him up against a small bank, and he clung on till the boat found him. On Monday, 31st August, I was washing down below, when the ship all of a sudden gave a tremendous lurch, and very nearly knocked me over. Bang she went again, every-one in an awful fright rolling all over the deck. Snap went the ropes we were towing the flat with, and in fact

I made certain we should be smashed to pieces. The fact was we had run aground, and the strong current coming down knocked us about tremendously. We succeeded at last in getting her off by backing, but still we left this bank before us, and it must be got through. No damage was done, except some sand got into the engines, so we had to anchor till they were cleaned. We then tried another channel and got through all safe to our great delight. I can't tell you what an unpleasant feeling it was, not like the rolling of a ship, because that is always regular, but this was a kind of quivering motion on the top of this bank, every moment expecting she would go quite over. She almost touched the water once, but not quite. On Wednesday, 2nd September, we arrived at Monghyr. This is a very curious place, but not a very nice one. We were close in shore to the town, and it was great fun watching the natives on shore. It was also very interesting to watch the fellows praying. They stand up to their hips in water (you know the Ganges is sacred to them), and then they sprinkle themselves all over, and look at the sun, muttering their prayers all the while. We only stayed here one afternoon, and started the next day. On Thursday, 3rd September, we had a man die from fever. The same afternoon we anchored in shore and buried him. It was a beautiful evening and a very imposing sight, the band in front playing the Dead March, and a company of men, with arms reversed, marching in the rear. We buried him in a beautiful looking place under some trees. I forgot to tell you on this day we were in sight of the Himalaya Mountains. On the 5th September we arrived at Dinapore, went to the barracks, and stayed there six days. The "Mirzapore" was a horrible steamer; she was all engines and most fearfully hot, with no room whatever for the men, consequently they were not healthy. At Dinapore we lost two men of cholera. On the 14th September we lost one man of cholera, on the 16th another one, on the 18th two more; so you see it was quite raging on board of her. The nine days we were on board of her there were six cases of cholera, of which four were fatal. There are 46 men on the diet list now, but they will soon get used they say to the climate. On the 18th of September there was a partial eclipse. They have made a breach in the walls of Delhi, and taken about half the town, with 600 men and 28 officers killed. All the Sepoys that are running away from Delhi will scatter all over the country, so I am afraid it will be a long job to kill them all. 250 Sepoys were captured the other day and tied to the muzzles of the guns and blown to pieces. "Sarved 'em right!" don't you think so, after murdering all the women and children? What humbug those dirks are, they are all very well to walk about Portsmouth with, but are no use for real fighting. I don't know what I shall do with mine against a Sepoy, but remember I have got a revolver. I can fire six times before he could fire three times, so I shall have a good enough chance. There are two flys attached to this house, and we make free use of them and have capital drives. I forgot to tell you that our old doctor, who belonged to the "Shannon," was taken such a fancy to by Lord Elgin when he was on board, that the former appointed him to his embassy as surgeon, so that we have got another surgeon who belonged to the 37th

Native Regiment, and he was fired upon when his regiment mutinied, but he got away all safe. He is now going up attached to the Naval Brigade. He is a very good doctor.

October 3rd.

The letter bag is to be closed to-day, so that I must finish my letter at once. All right, except a misfortune has happened to Mr. Bowman. Ninety rupees were stolen last night, and his desk broken open, and a fellow was seen going down to the river last night; they expect to bury it. They have caught a man and shut him up, but we don't know if he is the one. Lucknow is taken, with 400 men killed, including the great General Niel, so it is both bad and good news at the same time. Mr. Vaughan with the rest of the men are to be stationed at a place down the river called Buxar, so they will not join us. It is rumoured that we are to be stationed at Allahabad to protect it, but I don't think so. Captain Peel will be so savage if they keep him out of the fighting. To-day is Saturday, and we shall most likely start about Tuesday. I am not going to take my bearer up, but I will try and get one at Allahabad.

Give my best love to———, I hope he is all right. I felt for you very much on the 16th of September. Best love to all at and about Rockingham. I hope you are all quite strong and well. Good-bye.

Hoping this letter will reach you safe.

NAVAL BRIGADE,
CAMP NEAR CAWNPORE,
3rd December, 1857.

DEAR———

I have no time, so don't expect a long letter. Hoping you are all well, I will at once give you the news. I wrote to you about a fortnight ago, saying that we expected soon to go out and attack a large force called the Gwalior Contingent, numbered at least 16,000, with upwards of 40 guns. Well, on the 27th of November, we went out about two miles from the town (Cawnpore), and encamped with the rest of the forces under General Wyndham. At twelve o'clock that day, the enemy were reported advancing down upon us, so the alarm was sounded, and we all went to our posts. We (the Naval Brigade) had charge of two large 24-pounders, about 40 men, with one lieutenant, one mate, Lascelles and myself. The order came for us to move on, and on we went along the road with our two guns. We went on for about a mile and a half, when we met the enemy about 400 yards off on the road. We immediately began the action, with our guns banging away like bricks. Every now and then there was a cry "Look out, here's one for us," and I could see the flash and wiz-iz-iz, and down came a round shot slap along the road. Every now and then they sent us a volley of grape and cannister, and a man was wounded close by me. We pounded away at them for about half an hour, when the brutes got their guns all round us, so that as we turned our guns one way they pitched into us on the other, and we could not see any of them, except the gun on the road in front of us, as it was thickly wooded on both sides of the road, so we were obliged to retire and leave the guns, but not before the order came. As soon as we left them, the sailors scattered all over the place, some one way and some another, and we were not able to rally them, the bullocks having run away with the ammunition cart. Well, we gradually fell back, trying to rally the men, and the infantry then went up and we got the bullocks to the guns and took them back before the Sepoys could get hold of them, but I am sorry to say that the infantry got driven back also, and then it was a case of everyone for himself; officers and all got back as quick as they could, a tremendous fire pouring in on every side all the while. I saw one of our poor marines shot dead. We also ran back to the town, leaving our camp tents and all to the enemy, and retreated into the fort. Luckily, as soon as the alarm was given that we were retreating, my servant got all my things away from the chaplain's bungalow, where I was staying, and brought them into the fort. Here you see was my first action, a tremendous one, but a defeat, as the enemy were far too strong for us. All the 28th and 29th, we were being pounded into like fun, but we had plenty of guns in the fort and answering them briskly all day. The artillery officer gave me charge of a gun one afternoon, with some of our men, and we did just let fly at them. The only thing was we fired away almost all our ammunition. On the 29th, Lascelles and I were looking

over a parapet, when we saw a round shot kick up the
dust just outside, and over it came just over us. Lascelles
slipped and I bobbed to avoid it, and over we went both
of us together; such a jolly lark we had, and everyone
laughing at us. On the 30th, Sir Colin Campbell, from
Lucknow having heard the news of our being shut up,
arrived with a large force to our rescue, with jolly old
Captain Peel. As soon as ever he arrived, he got two
guns in position and began blazing away at them right
and left, and I can assure you it did one's heart good to
hear it. That afternoon the lieutenant came into the
fort to see us, and gave us an order to join the captain.
We were so glad to see him, and he was delighted at our
being in action. Lascelles and myself then joined him,
and we moved out to this camp, where the whole army
except those left in the fort are. We have fighting every
day. The day before yesterday we had tremendous
fighting in a narrow street and all through the town.
They say that the captain is much pleased with us, and
I hope I shall keep in his good graces. That day three
of our sailors' legs were taken off by a round shot. Since
then we have had no casualties. Every now and then
they send a shell or two and some round shot into our
camp, but have not done us much harm. The firing goes
on all through the night, and last night they tried to
make an attack, but were driven back by the 88th
regiment. Our lieutenant, who was commanding when
we went out to attack them, was wounded in three places;
but, thank God, I have not yet got a touch. I always
just say a little prayer to myself before going under
heavy fire, and then I never loose my pluck. It is indeed

a great cause of thankfulness that I have got through as far as this, and I hope you will all thank God especially for it and pray that I may be preserved through the rest. I suppose it will be this kind of work, fighting day and night for about five days more, when more troops will come up, and we shall all make a grand rush and drive them out of the place. It is quite a sight to see the captain under fire, he is so cool. He was leaning under a gun one morning, looking through a telescope, when a shell came and burst close to us, and he never even lifted his head, but kept looking through the glass all the while, and when a man behind us exclaimed that the bits were coming down like a shower of rain, he said "Nonsense, nonsense, it is only the dust and dirt!" I am getting quite used to the twang of the bullets now, and I hardly care about them at all, but the round shot I have a great dislike to. Two of our lieutenants have been promised the Victoria Cross for gallantry at Lucknow. The first shot I saw fired at us on the 27th made me think of you all, and what a different position I was in, but I soon got over that. When we were at the fort, before I joined the captain, we used to see the Sepoys running across the road about 200 yards off outside. They were all in uniform, and jackets and white trousers. These Gwalior contingents are very different from the Sepoys, and are splendid artillerymen, but I hope their day will soon come. Their making us run into the fort has given them extra pluck. Most of the ladies from Lucknow are here now, and the brutes have found out the place, and fire into them tremendously and into the hospital. It was a fearful thing to see the wounded coming in when we were in the fort, some with legs off and others with arms off, and some in the agonies of death. When once we get hold of these fellows won't we just drive them out of it. They are in thousands in the town hiding and sneaking about. We got our gun one day at the bottom of a narrow street, face to face with one of theirs at the top, but before they could fire at us, we began with our rifles and every now and then let them have it with our big gun. We made them leave their gun, and apparently there it was alone in the middle of the street, but the cunning brutes had a rope made fast to it, and dragged it away without exposing themselves, but every now and then a bold fellow took a look at us, but he got such an unpleasant reception he was obliged to retreat as quickly as he could. I have just been to tell our first lieutenant to open fire from his battery, and that place being a long way off, and the sun very hot, I am rather tired, and for that reason I must leave off. Weather very cold at night, tremendously hot in the day. Getting on all right.

NAVAL BRIGADE,
CAMP NEAR CAWNPORE,
December 11th, 1857.

DEAR ——

I hope you have received my last letter from here, telling you I had received yours dated 5th October, and giving you an account of my first action. I have now to give you an account of another one. I think I left off in my last letter at the 30th November, when I joined Captain Peel's part of the Naval Brigade that had just come up from Lucknow, and encamped with them about two miles to the left of the town, where I write from. Well, the next day, 1st December, we began operations immediately, fighting in the town (but I think I told you all about that day when we were nearly taking a gun, and three or four men had their legs taken off, so I will not say anything more about it here.) On the 2nd December, we stayed in our tents quietly all day, although there was a great deal of fighting going on, but we had no orders to do anything. That night the enemy had the impertinence to attack our camp on the right, but were soon sent about their business by the 88th and 44th regiments. On the 3rd December, about ten o'clock, the enemy got a gun in position, somewhere hidden in the town, and opened fire right slap into our camp. The round shot came in close to our tent, and it made it all the more disagreeable as we were not fighting them. If we had been out to them we should of course have expected it, but being quietly fired at while we were lying down in our tents was rather unpleasant as you may suppose, but we opened fire with one of our guns from a battery, and he very soon left off. That night we had to be ready, and so cold it was, as an attack was again expected. The bullocks were got in the guns, and everything ready, and then we turned in again and slept in our clothes, but I suppose the enemy had seen us getting ready, and thought better of it, as nothing at all happened. On the 4th December, there was a very little fighting to what there usually had been, and we heard that some of the enemy were crossing over the river into Oude. On the 5th December it was pretty quiet in the morning, but in the afternoon the enemy made a tremendous attack. I went with the captain to the other side of the river, with two of our large guns, and pitched into them right and left, and the attack was repulsed again all right. On this day they also tried to set fire to the bridge of boats, which is the only way we have of crossing the river, but they could not manage it. We also heard that the next day was fixed for a general attack to drive the brutes all out of the town. Now for it! 6th December. Early that morning we had just woke up in our tent, when an order came to strike tents immediately. Up we all got, put our things in the hackeray and everything ready. The men were made to fall in and everything done. The captain called Lascelles and me up privately and said we were going to make the grand attack, and that we were not to run and blow and go head over heels and to get out of breath, but to take it coolly. Well, about nine o'clock, we moved with three 24-pounders, one 8-inch howitzer, and two rockets, leaving two guns in camp, and two at a battery. We halted when we had gone some way, and waited for the troops. There were the 93rd Highlanders, 43rd ditto, 53rd and 23rd were the principle regiments. When everything was ready we moved on first, with the guns away to the left. We soon got in sight of the enemy. There they all were, shoals upon shoals of them, most of them half hidden among the jungles. We moved on, Captain Peel riding ahead to show the way for some time in sight of the enemy without their firing a single shot, which I wondered at very much. We got our guns in the position laid down and opened fire. There were we quite by ourselves in a large plain, with only the 53rd regiment for our support, the whole army drawn up about a quarter of a mile behind us in one long line. We then opened fire, giving them the first shot, and they soon answered us. Captain Peel went galloping about all over the place, so I could but run after him like a groom. He told me to stick by the gun, our first lieutenant was commanding, and to stay with him for the present. We blazed away for some time as hard as we could, they giving us shot for shot, and bursting their shells beautifully. But this did not last long. Our Marines and the 53rd charged, and at the same time we gave them two rockets slap into the middle of them, and then with three good cheers we advanced our guns, and they actually ran. Didn't we just yell and shout. On we went up a road where they had two guns in position, and they gave us a tremendous fire, and a good many stood their ground and gave us volley after volley of

musketry. I expected to see some of our men drop every
minute, but no. The shot and shell came within an ace
of us, but not one touched us. On we went, the brutes
saw us still advancing, and off they took their guns. On
came our infantry, and we fairly set them running.
Captain Peel now dismounted, and I went with him, and
we came over a bridge on the road which went through a
field crowded with Sepoys. I can't tell you how jolly it
was seeing the brutes run. I hardly could believe my
eyes. I felt perfectly mad, and our men got on the top
of the guns waving their hats and cheering and yelling
like fun; it was most awfully exciting. We pursued
them to the camp, found it all deserted; tents, horses,
ponies, baggage, bedding, swords, muskets, everything
lying about, hackerays, loaded with all manner of treasure
all left. On we went still right through the camp, and
after them across the fields and roads at a tremendous
pace. I got fairly out of breath, and the only way I
could keep up when I was on a message from the captain,
out of hearing, was to say to myself "Hoiks over, Hoiks
over, fox ahead!" and I used to go along double the pace.
We chased them for about ten miles along the road to
Calpee, when we got ordered to halt. We took seventeen
guns, loads upon loads of ammunition, all their luggage,
treasures, and everything—there's for you. I could have
got anything almost if I had chosen to pick it up. Money
was lying about the road, clothing of all kinds, and almost
every imaginable thing you could think of. The panic was
taken by those who were in the town, and they all hooked
up as hard as they could do, so we got the place quite
clean of them. We returned quite late that night and

bivouaced close to the place where the enemy had their camp. The first lieutenant, Lascelles, and I slept under a captured gun as comfortably as possible. Captain Peel was so delighted, he says that the battle is the death blow to the rebellion. The next day a pursuing column was sent up the country, consisting of cavalry and horse artillery. They found the enemy at a place called Bithoor, some way up the river, where they were trying to cross. They didn't try to fight this time, but left fifteen more guns in our hands, and lots more luggage. Most of them threw down their arms and jumped into the river. So much for the Gwalior contingent: I think they have been pretty well settled. We have stayed in the camp since then. Our tents came up the next day, and we have not heard what our next move will be. The only thing in the way of loot I have got is a small flag, one of their camp colors, and two brass plates belonging to some of their regiments, which they wear on their caps. As we were chasing them up the road, we passed a hackeray with a lot of bundles underneath, and some of our men happened I suppose to give them a kick, but anyhow, up jumped a Sepoy. One of our men drew his cutlass and soon settled him. I have no doubt he thought himself very cunning and clever to hide under there. So you see from 27th November to 6th December I hardly passed a day without being under fire, and yet, thank God, I have not been touched once.

We get on very well here, although the white ants eat right through our mattresses and bedding, so that we had to give up sleeping on the ground, and we have each got a wooden bedstead to sleep on, which makes our tent look quite comfortable.

www.ingramcontent.com/pod-product-compliance
Lightning Source LLC
Chambersburg PA
CBHW020911090426
42736CB00008B/582